THE SCALPEL AND THE KUKRI

A Surgeon and his family's adventures among the Gurkhas

PETER PITT

PETER PITT

Printed in Great Britain
by Antony Rowe Ltd.,
Chippenham, Wiltshire
SN14 6LH

0-9552059-0-5
978-0-9552059-0-3

Contents

PHOTOGRAPHS

AUTHOR'S NOTE

I dedicated my first book, "Surgeon in Nepal", to the British Tax Payer.

I devote this present effort to the Royal Army Medical Corps (R.A.M.C.) and the Queen Alexandra's Royal Army Nursing Corps (Q.A.R.A.N.C) without whose assistance, I could never have managed these problems.

I am not an authority on Nepal and what I have learned is from 2 years spent only at the British Military Hospital, where my chief interpreter and informant was Hemlata - a dedicated and highly intelligent Tibetan Auxiliary Nurse, in the Out Patient Department.

I started my first book by buying a box of 24 tins of Tiger beer. Emptying the box proved no problem. I then had the container for the story. Whenever I experienced an event of interest, I recorded the details that same evening, dropping my findings into the box. The hardest time was during the monsoon when my forearm stuck to the paper in the high humidity. I had to peel the sheet off my arm.

George Douglas, a Nepalese – Scottish artist, who lived in Darjeeling, illustrated the book, insisting on absolute authenticity. John Murray published it in 1970.

These are the second part of our adventures – mentioning some of my mistakes

I would like to thank my brother Brice for his advice, especially on what I should "bin".

I apologise to you – the reader – for my not taking all Brice's advice!

I was 32 when we arrived in Nepal and graded a Senior Specialist (equivalent to Senior Registrar).

I had previously served as a military surgeon in Nigeria, when 28, and eventually graded Specialist (Registrar). I was invited to act as honorary surgeon at the civilian hospital in Kaduna, whenever I had time – halcyon days for an unattached surgeon.

Earlier, I had assisted my father, Norman Pitt and tried to copy his skills but with little practical experience until the 18 month tour in West Africa.

All I have learned is from Father, a brilliant technical surgeon, who taught me the art of surgery:

to be gentle

to minimise blood loss

to be quick and decisive.

In later years I have tried to add "pain control", (by injecting bupivacaine with adrenaline, before commencing an operation).

Most importantly, **thank you Michelle** for always remaining so resourceful, cheerful and enthusiastic, even at the end of a fifty plus hour week, to complete this book.

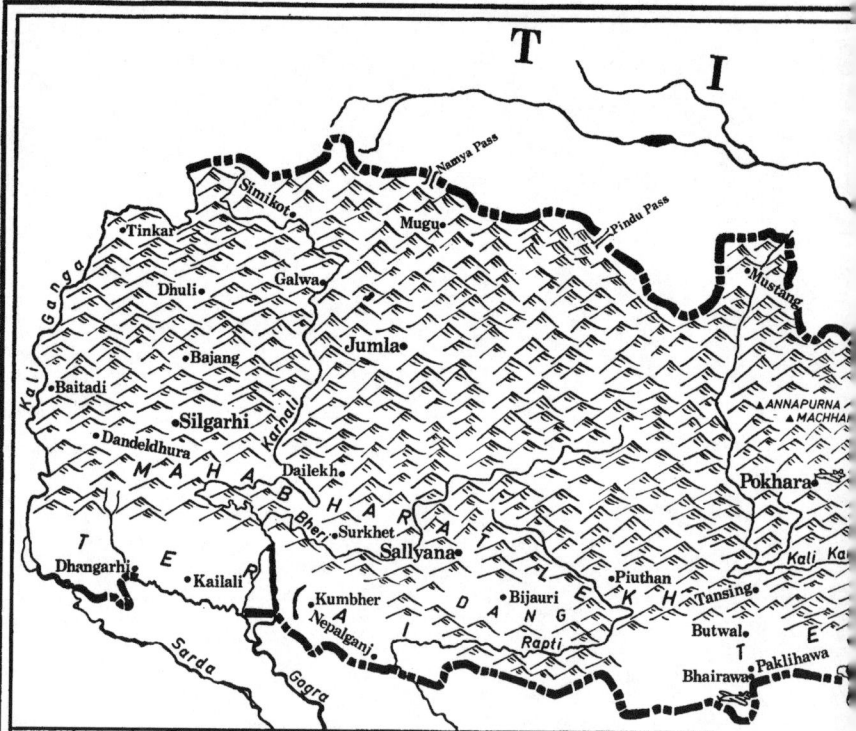

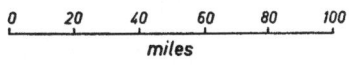

FOREWORD

By Brigadier A. B. Taggart M. C.

Major Peter Pitt was the surgeon at the British Military hospital in Dharan, East Nepal, when I was commanding the Gurkha Recruiting Depots in Nepal in the 1960's.

Although the hospital was relatively small, it had to cater for Gurkha soldiers serving in the depots as well as those on leave in Nepal and, of course, for British staff and their families. Inevitably, it was also constantly having to deal with retired soldiers and their families who used to come to Dharan for a wide variety of medical problems. At that time, there were almost no roads in the mountain areas of Nepal, and virtually no medical centres anywhere except in the larger towns. So those, servicemen or not, who came to seek medial help, had walked, or been carried, for several days before reaching Dharan, and any help for their health problems.

Peter and his staff always did what they could, within the limits imposed, by higher authority, on their activities, to help anyone of these unfortunates; their assistance made an invaluable contribution to maintaining the goodwill of all the hill people in the surrounding areas – whether military or not – and the Brigade of Gurkhas was certainly very grateful for that.

I look forward to seeing Peter's new book which will, I am sure, give a very interesting account not only of the work he and his staff did in Nepal but also of life in general there in the 1960's.

Tony Taggart

MICHAEL PALIN

To Peter — *[handwritten: best wishes]*

[signature]

Book signing, following Michael's address to a packed house, at the Royal Society of Medicine, No.1. Wimpole St, London, W1G 0AE on June 2nd 2005.

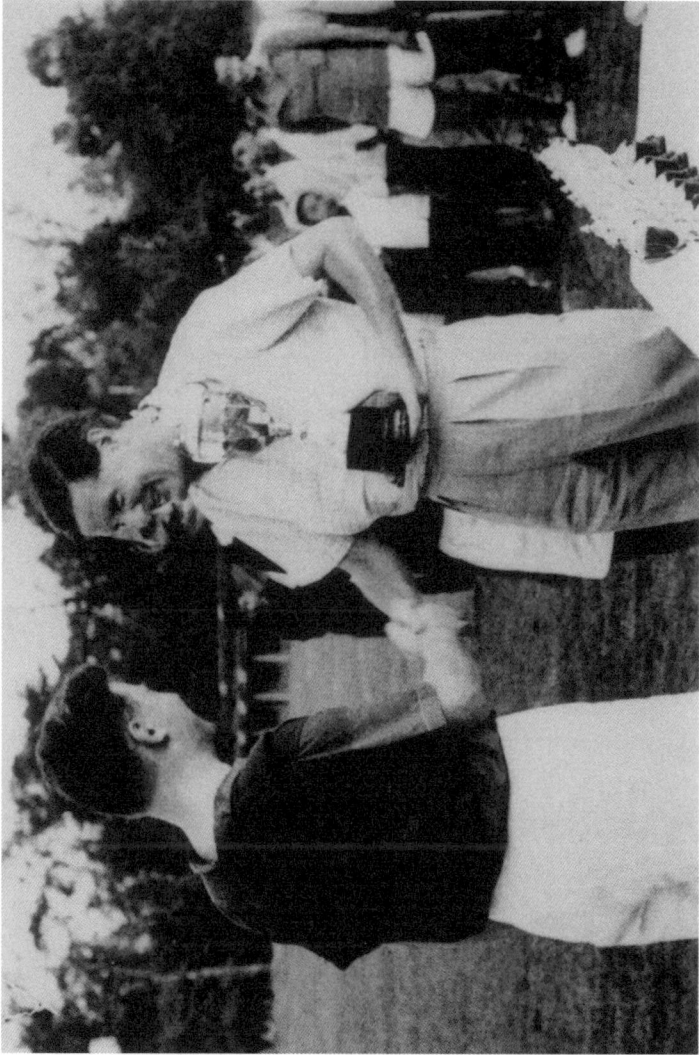

BRIGADIER TAGGART PRESENTING INTER-HOCKEY CUP TO AUTHOR

THE HOSPITAL TEAM, WITH MAJOR MIKE BANAHAN AND RANJIT RAI

INTRODUCTION

Village children playing with home made toys

CHAPTER 1

Burns

Twenty-five year old Maipal had been taking a load of wood in a three ton lorry from Dharan to Biratnager. With him was his <u>dhobi</u>, his washerman. Now although Maipal was aware of his leaking petrol cap, he hadn't realised that a smouldering forest fire had reached quite so close to the road.

Suddenly, he had to pull off the central tarmac on to the rougher buffalo track, by the side of the road, to avoid a head-on collision. This sudden jerk caused more fuel to spill which a spark ignited. In a flash, the lorry was in flames.

Maipal leapt on the brakes but in the seconds it took to bring the vehicle to a halt, he was burned beyond any hope of recovery. Well over sixty per cent of his body was charred (*no one with burns of over 40% ever survived in Nepal*). His eyes were burned beyond recognition. He was in a pathetic, pitiful state.

The terrified <u>dhobi,</u> (this is how he opted to be addressed,) had jumped from the still-moving vehicle and was last seen by eye-witnesses fleeing, screaming, into the jungle. As he ran, he tore at his burning clothes, ripping them from him. For two and a half days we were to hear no more of him.

Meanwhile Maipal was taken to Judhanager Hospital, the tiny ten bedded government hospital in Dharan, where he was covered with Gentian Violet, a dye that does little good, besides staining the tissue and microorganisms that come in contact with it. From there, he was sent up to the British Military Hospital (B.M.H), but the problem was beyond us too.

The successful management of severe burns is a highly-skilled operation, requiring first-class laboratory facilities, expert nursing and a team of expert specialists. These we could not provide. More important still, is the need for plasma, serum is lost by the pint in a case of severe burns. We had none, having long since exhausted our meagre supply. Instead, I gave him all the compatible blood from the little store that I had spent three weeks building up.

It was all to no avail. The dreaded complication of severe shock set in. It follows a few hours after such ghastly burns and results in renal failure. He needed an artificial kidney. There is no such machine in Nepal; I doubt if there was even one in India. I cut down the fluid "intake" to an absolute minimum, praying that the kidneys might recover; but it was not to be. A perfectly fit twenty-five year old died in a few days..... and his colleague? Well, he ran and ran through the jungle. Soon he had ripped off all his clothes, but the ghastly pain was more that he could bear. Finally he stumbled into a forest stream and drank buckets of the muddy water, for he was consumed by a terrible thirst. This was the best thing he could possibly have done. It lessened dehydration and diminished the likelihood of shock. He rolled up in leaves under a great sal tree and collapsed into a deep, exhausted sleep, oblivious to any leopard that might be on the prowl.

Next day, he stumbled through the forest, until he arrived at a little farm on the outskirts, where Dilbahadur and Ganeshkumari Chettri lived. He was able to borrow some old clothes from the railway worker to cover his nakedness.

It was nearly sixty hours since his accident before I actually saw him. I had heard about him, but assumed he must have died. An ex-Gurkha major, now a recruiting officer, was returning home through the jungle, after working on his farm, when he found the man sitting by the side of the road. He sent an urgent signal to the hospital. I dispatched the ambulance to the jungle. I knew his condition couldn't be as desperate as Maipal's for, if it had, he would be dead. The lad was in a filthy state, covered in mud. I couldn't even see how severe his burns were.

I try never to cut clothing for this might be all they own. However, I didn't hesitate long before ripping off Dilbahadur's rags. Fortunately earth is a great deal easier to wash off than Gentian Violet and after the dhobi had had a long bath, I was relieved to find that his burns looked relatively minor – and hoped he might escape skin grafting. Meanwhile Maipal died, a little over twenty-four hours after his companion had been admitted.

It is very difficult to determine the severity of even superficial burns in the first few days. Almost without exception, they are worse than they first appear. The same was true with the dhobi. His arms and legs did in fact require fairly extensive grafting. He was with us several weeks before going home, a fit man – physically at least.

*   *   *   *   *

During March, the dead leaves tend to fall and by April these and the parched grass are burned and the forest seemed gently to smoulder. It is so dry that I could never understand why it did not errupt into flames, for unexpected winds suddenly blew up with tremendous force. During these months, the mountains behind the hospital looked most attractive at night, as whole columns of fire lit up the darkness; the ground is deliberately burned prior to planting maize, which springs up as the monsoon breaks in June. Nothing ever happened in Nepal without some tragic consequence.

Little Harkabahadur (*Bahadur is easily the commonest first name in Nepal, meaning "warrior"*) was everyone's darling. Though severely burned when only three weeks old, I did not see him until fifteen months later. By then his right arm had fixed solidly down the side of his body with his tiny hand in the "porter's tip" position. The arm was useless because, as rarely used, had only partially developed. He didn't even have an elbow, as his upper arm and forearm had fused together.

I succeeded in freeing his arm. He never once cried following the operation. He was so thrilled with it. He kept putting objects into his "newly found" hand, and showed literally everyone who came to the ward his new acquisition. We had to perform three or four further operations to get the wrist completely straight, as the burn contracture had been so severe that the side of his little finger had been at one with the wrist.

I'm afraid he left hospital a very spoilt little boy but he did have a presentable arm, with which he clutched his favourite toy. This was an intravenous transfusion bag.

When these disposable polythene bags are empty, they can be blown up and sealed by knotting the tubing leading from the bag. This results in a soft football, a cuddly and floating toy or anything else a child's mind can conjure up. Certainly Harkabahadur could never be tempted far from his five per cent dextrose bag.

*   *   *   *   *

The monsoon season ends at the beginning of October and from November it is distinctly chilly. The rains usually return briefly at Christmas but from then on the danger of fire increases with the cold and drought. The houses are constructed almost entirely of timber and a single spark, caught by a sudden gust, could be enough to destroy an entire village. Tragically, there are many villagers bearing the hall-mark of these fires; how many more have succumbed, one could never guess.

Surgery is not always successful. Dhurbahadur had been only five years old when he was seriously burned while pathetically trying to save his mother in one of these fires; both parents died that night. His face had been so badly damaged that, as the wounds healed, his lower lip had been pulled right down inside out, so that, at a distance, it looked as if he was sticking out his tongue; close to, he looked grotesque. His teeth had been permanently exposed, so that they were decayed and deformed. This added to the macabre appearance. We performed multiple operations, including a tracheostomy, so that he could breathe through his neck, as the inside of his mouth and throat had been so badly scarred that he was in danger of suffocating. Because of the deformities, it had become impossible to anaesthetise him. The endotracheal tube would simply not enter the windpipe. His heart stopped twice on the operating table, as the anaesthetist struggled in vain to intubate. Twice he had been resuscitated by external cardiac massage, performed by repeated pressure on the chest, jerking the heart back to life, while flooding in oxygen through the mask.

We had to perform major skin grafting procedures under local anaesthetic – far too distressing on one so young. Our results were disappointing, to say the least.

Sadly, all I could eventually do was send him home - I fear to succumb from either pneumonia or tuberculosis, but I was never to find out.

CHAPTER 2

Jewellery

Amba was so proud of her heavy gold ring, passed down to her, when her pensioner father died. (He had been presented with it by a British Gurkha officer). She had been to the market and was returning home in the early evening, carrying her loaded basket. It had started to rain heavily, causing her to slip off the mountain path. She grabbed at a broken branch but her ring was trapped on the trunk, as she crashed unceremoniously down the mountain side, aggravated by the weight of her basket. Her ring and flesh were ripped off, much like pulling a finger out of a glove, leaving only bare bone. Her head struck a rock and she blacked out. She was discovered next morning and carried to us – with a sad little bundle – her ring and finger. Sadly, amputation of the finger was the only practical treatment I could offer for what is called a degloving injury.

*   *   *   *   *

Most of the women and even some of the boys have pierced ears; a number wear little gold earrings. Netrabahadur, when five, had been racing through the jungle in some game of hide and seek, when a branch slipped through his earring and ripped it off. For the next fifteen years, the torn lobe of his ear had hung down and caused him considerable embarrassment and irritation. It was a relatively simple job to repair and I thought how clever I had been, when I put a little orange stick in the wound, to prevent the lobe sealing completely, thus healing with the original hole. All seemed well until he presented, a mere three days later, at my Out-Patients

Department. I twisted the little piece of wood to stop the tissue adhering to it. He looked very glum. He didn't like it at all! I explained again why I had put it there and that it would need only remain a few more days. Apparently he now no longer wanted his ears pierced, as he had been teased so much by his friends. I simply removed the little stick and he went home delighted. Fortunately the hole was there ,so he would still be able to wear a ring, if he changed his mind.

A Gurkha soldier's wife – sporting her jewellery

Bhagirathi told me that she wanted her nose repaired. I studied it carefully before exclaiming "But I can't see anything wrong!" At that she looked up and I noticed how the fleshy portion between the two nostrils was split. The heavy gold nasal ring, the n*akphul*, ("nose flower"), had gradually worn through over the years, until finally it had dropped out, a month earlier. She didn't really care about her nose, only that she could no longer wear her jewellery! I promised I would repair the tissue but warned that she mustn't wear her ring for at least three months – I didn't want it to break down again. A week after the operation, I spotted her in the market, wearing the *nakphul*!

CHAPTER 3

Gun Shot Wound

Fifteen year old Kharkabahadur lived with his brothers in a little cluster of houses by the forest, a day's journey from the hospital. Now, villagers do not bother with such luxuries as lavatories and the male dress of voluminous trousers is not designed for micturition in the Western style. Kharkabahadur entered the bushes, squatted down to pass water in the normal Nepalese fashion. As he rose, a bullet smashed through his left knee. He was so astonished that he felt little initial pain. He turned to see a man fleeing through the trees. We never discovered why he shot Kharkabahadur. He had only been ten yards away and had used a rifle. We assumed he had been poaching and fled when he realised what he had hit was human not animal: it was early July, very much the closed season when, mating over, the offspring were still very young. Kharkabahadur's brothers collected him and carried him in a basket, on their shoulders to the hospital.

He arrived over twenty-four hours after the accident. His left knee was grossly swollen. There was an entry wound on the outside, the same size as the exit wound on the inside – an odd finding, following a high velocity injury, except perhaps when the bullet simply cuts through soft tissue. Normally there is such a small entry wound, that can easily be missed and a huge exit hole.

As I pieced together his story with the appearance of his wounds, I realised just how lucky Kharkabahadur had been. If he had been squatting a second more, the bullet would have passed through his heart. As it was, it had gone so accurately through his knee that it was almost uncanny. It had travelled through the front of the joint, opening up the same "safe" areas which surgeons used to incise to remove torn cartilages and loose bodies. Thus neither the femur, tibia nor patella (knee-cap) had been damaged. Most of the vessels to the leg pass through the back of the knee, all these were undamaged, and even the nerve that winds its way round the head of the fibula, on the outside of the knee, had been untouched; without this nerve, Kharkabahadur would never have been able to walk normally, for he would have had to drag a dangling foot for the rest of his life.

So what harm had the bullet done? It had damaged the inside of his knee joint and blasted a piece of cartilage almost out through the exit hole. This meant that, though Kharkabahadur might escape with a painless knee, he would probably develop osteo-arthritis in the years to come, though this could be many years hence, a small sacrifice for his life.

His brothers had stopped the haemorrhage by rubbing sindur into both wounds.

When I got the lad to theatre, I cut away the dead skin round the holes, evacuated blood clots and removed the piece of cartilage.

Suturing gun-shot wounds is tantamount to disaster, so we simply sprayed his knee with an antibiotic powder and prescribed Penicillin and Streptomycin to minimise infection. As always, I prescribed Anti Tetanus Serum (A.T.S) to prevent tetanus.

When I saw him next day he was much happier. I asked what the poacher might have been after. He explained that tiger, bear, jungle-fowl and peafowl frequent that part of the jungle. He felt he would not be able to recognise the poacher as he had not seen him clearly.

The knee healed better that I could have hoped; already he had practically regained full movement and was walking painlessly by the time he left hospital. The outlook was vastly better than I had at first feared.

This was the country to which I had brought Anna with James, my three-month old baby, some weeks earlier, to be the only surgeon at the British Military Hospital for the next two years. I had first written about my experiences there in 1970 and these further reminiscences, recollected in 2005, complete my narrative.

OUTWARD BOUND

A rabid jackal attacking a Gurkha cantonment guard,
who is about to draw his Kukri.
"Better to die than to be a coward".

CHAPTER 4

The Journey Out

We left England in the middle of April 1966, on the coldest day that month in the previous thirty five years, with over half the country snowbound; we arrived at Dum Dum where the temperature was 35 °C at 10.00am and rose to 41 °C, with a humidity of 95% in the afternoon, the hottest recorded so far that year in Calcutta! Our two years in Nepal were about to begin.

I had sent off the crates two months earlier and another, filled with last minute purchases, a few days before we flew. We had to wait six months for these to arrive! About a fortnight earlier, the Army had informed me that, as we were to fly economy class on a B.O.A.C. jet, where the weight allowance was 44lbs, our total would be 132lbs. (They gave Anna and me an extra 22lbs each, to bring ours up to the first class allowance, though they wouldn't run to the actual cost of the seats). James was allowed the weight of his carrycot! Previously they had promised 246lbs, the amount on an RAF chartered flight. The loss of these 114lbs had made the last fortnight a misery, as we had previously weighed everything to the promised amount. It was equivalent to two very heavy large suitcases, and a severe blow. One hundred and thirty two pounds wasn't much to take to such an isolated country – and it seemed very little indeed, as we waited for the crates to arrive.

We were not, however, going to be beaten. We put all the baby's napkins – a prodigious number – and clothes under the mattress of a wicker carry cot. (Anna had chosen this, so that air could circulate; we thought that the baby would be far too uncomfortable in a plastic cot). We then put the baby's toys on top and thus retrieved 22lbs.

I had double pockets to my overcoat; these Anna's mother, Betty Pratt, elongated some six inches into "poacher's pockets", so that they would take twice as much. She did the same with Anna's coat. I then stuffed these with items I thought I would be unable to buy in Nepal: batteries for the transistor radio and clock, packets of seeds, plugs and adaptors, deodorants and lipstick. I looked like a walking Christmas tree, as the side pockets of my suit were similarly crammed, accentuating the overcoat still further.

At Heathrow, my heart sank. I noted that the carrycot was larger than the official dimentions. But the officers, at the weighing counter, ignored the disparity. In addition, they did not weigh the luggage I was going to take on the plane, just the two suitcases, tape recorder and gun for the Officers' mess. I even had two kilograms weight allowance in reserve for the onward flight to Nepal. I had taken the precaution of putting the major part of our accompanied luggage out of sight!

We had a duffle bag full of toilet necessities for the baby, two large plastic bags of hand luggage, containing items for the journey: slacks and bedroom slippers, two hats (one an enormous Caribbean sun-hat for Anna), an umbrella, a cine and still camera, a large bundle of that day's papers and magazines (as we thought these might be the last we would read for two years), Anna's handbag and a thermos bag. (The newspapers were very welcome though the overseas edition of the Daily Telegraph did arrive routinely to be passed from home to home).

Moving all this proved a nightmare, especially when the hostesses tried to carry the terribly top-heavy carrycot. They then offered "at least to carry a coat!" Somehow we got the baby aboard, though, as I stumbled on the steep gangway, one of the bags slipped from under my arm and crashed to the ground. Another visibly wilted, as she tried to retrieve it before I could dump James, practically thrown out of the cot, in my agitation to get there first!

Our carrycot was quite impractical. James was transferred to the "sky" cot slotted onto the partition, between first and economy class. We stowed ours on a shelf at the back. Our allocation on the Boeing 707, was two of three seats crammed together. We were most unlucky, as this was a £10 emigration flight to Australia without a spare seat available.

Twice more I fought my way the length of the plane, down the crowded gangway, back to the lounge to collect more luggage. "I don't know how they let you take all this on with you," sighed a harassed airhostess. I was past caring, my concern being to load up before the gangway was taken down, with, ideally, me on board...... I felt terribly sorry for the New Zealander seated in the aisle seat, as I kept squeezing past him.

Having got everything neatly packed in the overhead shelves, we were politely but firmly told to take down all heavy objects – which consisted of everything, apart from the hats! This was a great deal easier to be asked, than do, because there is absolutely no leg room. At this time, I was only vaguely aware of what is now known as "economy class syndrome". According to Alaistair Cooke in his "Letter From America", in 2003, between 250,000 and 500,000 passengers a year suffer a deep vein thrombosis, from which a number die. These days I wear the stockings provided when undergoing an operation, try to walk around the plane as much as possible and drink plenty of water.

Pieces of our luggage were soon distributed throughout the length and breadth of the 707. During the flight, I was handed a box of films, this added to the bulk. I couldn't even sit, let alone fasten the safety belt! Instead, I held it across, pretending it had been, until airborne. Then I filled a large plastic bag. As I emptied my pockets, I felt somewhat liberated. I could at least sit. We added smaller packages to the bag to reduce the number. The result, when we disembarked at Dum Dum, was more like Father Christmas, with this huge bag slung over my shoulder, than the "Christmas tree" that had boarded at Heathrow!

During the flight, I had become good friends with our companion; a diplomatic move, for soon, as our luggage seeped towards the gangway, he had no leg room either! Still, at least he could stretch his legs into the aisle and would be free of us at Calcutta.

He and his wife had flown to England three weeks earlier; their daughter dying from renal failure in spite of dialysis. They had reached her a week before the end.

Our plane stopped at Frankfurt, Beirut and Karachi. I had got off at each stop but Anna was stuck on board the whole flight. Beirut was fascinating, but I hadn't realised I had first to collect a boarding card. At the airport I argued frantically to get back. I had the passports, Anna had the tickets. My protestations failed so I simply ducked under the official's arm and ran back to the plane, hoping I wouldn't be shot!

Whisky was £1 a bottle with electrical goods very cheap. I couldn't even contemplate a purchase as there was nowhere to put it.

Anna was breast feeding and nursing curtains were hooked around her whenever a feed was due. This added to the burden of the hostesses. Fortunately he was the only baby.

"I shouldn't wear that overcoat if I were you, Sir," smiled the hostess, as we landed at Calcutta. "Its over a hundred degrees, (38 °C) Sir." Little did she know it was <u>still</u> too heavy to carry! All I now cared about was collecting everything.

CHAPTER 5

Calcutta

The grave of a young family who perished in the smallpox epidemic.
Their clothes, toys and feeding utensils are left for the next world.

At Dum Dum, we somehow managed to get everything into the Customs Hall, where the first thing I did was strip down to my shirt. James had turned as red as a lobster, sweating visibly but remained sleeping. Anna collapsed on to a hard bench.

In my haste to catch up with the luggage, I had walked straight past the "Health" and "Passport" desks. Fortunately we were met by a very helpful staff sergeant from the Movements section of the British Army. We showed our certificates of smallpox and cholera vaccination at the health desk; he hardly bothered to look at them and had anyway already let us pass without a murmur. We then handed in our disembarkation cards, which I had completed with my fountain pen coated in ink, as this invariably leaks on high altitude flights. My inky fingers, added to my sweaty hands, made them pretty well indecipherable.

The Customs officer listened attentively to all I declared. It was quite a sight to see our luggage filling the entire bench. He impounded the rifle; I had no intention in taking that through Calcutta.

We were met by Anna's doctor friend, Adi Gazder, a paediatrician in Calcutta, he had been Anna's father's, (Bill Pratt) house surgeon at Willsden General, years earlier and whose wife, Daphne Spottiswood, a concert pianist, had lived with the Pratts a considerable period.

Adi immediately wanted confirmation that James had been vaccinated. I explained that he was not yet three months and that the best authority I could find had advised us not to vaccinate him until nine months, as the risk of encephalitis (inflammation of the brain) and vaccinia might be more serious than the disease. In addition, he was being breast fed and Anna herself had only recently been successfully vaccinated. (Antibodies would pass to James through her milk.) He told me that I had been given bad advice and that all babies in Calcutta are vaccinated in their first few weeks, this being an endemic area. He warned that I must keep the baby in the house and not take him anywhere until he had been. Calcutta was not safe, as infested dust could theoretically infect the child. I felt suitably chastened. When I arrived in Nepal, I was greeted by the same lecture from the surgeon, Jim Arnott, I was taking over from. (Nearly a thousand people were known to have died in the previous three months in the villages around the hospital in Nepal. For many months after, corpses of villagers, who had died in the epidemic, were discovered in the jungle.)

I immediately vaccinated James on arrival in Nepal. Nothing happened. A pustule has to form at the site of the needle prick. Even though I repeated this at frequent intervals, it did not "take" until he was 9 months, for he was truly getting sufficient protection through Anna. Up to that time, however, I had to ensure that he was only handled by people whom I knew had been vaccinated and therefore not a health hazard. Ironically he did suffer vaccinia, but only like a very mild case of chicken pox.

From Dum Dum, we sped in the doctor's chauffeur-driven Ambassador - all cars in Calcutta seem to be Ambassadors! - along a few miles of dual carriage-way; our luggage followed in an Army landrover. Tall palm trees made the view pleasantly tropical. At first Adi had the windows wound down and a cool breeze blew through the car. All was comfortable apart from the occasional bump, as we hit the odd pothole.

Suddenly the peace was shattered - the dual carriage-way had ended. Adi had all the windows closed. Noisy squatters had built flimsy shelters right in the middle of the road! A shanty town had mushroomed up like some malignant growth. The hovels were like giant playing cards, so thin were their wicker walls, held together by mud; the squalor had to be seen to be believed. On our return, two years later, the colony had grown even bigger. No government, I was informed by Adi, had sufficient courage to clear it. Soon we were in the middle of Calcutta. The driving was not only atrocious but incredibly noisy, horns blasting continuously, with the result that no one takes a blind bit of notice. I was sure we must hit something, but at the last second, a collision was averted, if only by an inch or two. I was sick with terror, noise and the heat. Adi, however, sat completely unruffled, quite oblivious to it all.

He explained that, whatever happened, we must not harm a cow - far better hit a pedestrian than injure a sacred animal. There must be a million of these wandering across the streets, munching snatched vegetables from the stalls. Thousands were sitting sunning themselves on the main road, while another had her calf across her shoulders. If however, we were to hit a pedestrian, the local populace would immediately blame us, whoever was at fault. The "vehicle" is always the culprit, and as likely as not, they would turn the car over and set it alight. This explanation hardly added to the enjoyment of the drive!

People were washing in holes in the pavement and a child was happily taking a shower from water cascading on to the street through a broken water pipe.

Adi had sacrificed his air-conditioned bedroom to us. Entering was paradise. When I left for a few minutes to talk with the doctor, while Anna was feeding James, I found the heat insufferable. I hadn't really noticed the temperature with the anxieties of the move, but now ....! I quickly downed the beer Adi had provided and slunk back into the blessed coolness.

At this time there had been much in the English press of starvation and food riots in Calcutta. We saw no evidence of lawlessness. It is an amazing city: seething masses of humanity everywhere, with the stench of cooking revolting. Yet you can get the best food in the world. There is also great wealth, and some of the shops Adi took us to were as smart as any in the West End. The fashion houses were full of exotic fabrics and silks and the bigger stores were air conditioned, a wonderful incentive for long and relaxing shopping!

We were to spend a hectic three days: cocktail parties, dinners, sightseeing and visiting temples. How we managed in our unacclimatised state, in that heat, I cannot now imagine!

CHAPTER 6

Our Arrival

Our introduction to Nepal was not a happy one. The plane had been due to fly at 6.00 am and we had been instructed to be there an hour earlier. Adi knew the airlines better and felt 5.30 quite soon enough. We set off from his house at 4.30 and were at the Royal Nepalese Airline counter, half an hour later, yet the only sign of life was a couple of porters as they snored loudly.

I shook one of the men, who grudgingly got up and put our cases on the weighing machine. That done, he went back to sleep. Finally at 6.00 am, when the plane was actually due to depart, an unwashed, unshaven and half-asleep officer arrived. The Movements Sergeant paid for the luggage, with our "excess baggage voucher". The B.O.A.C. ticket covered virtually 100lbs.

I collected the gun and waited impatiently till 7.00 am, when we were at least allowed to see the plane. We watched while all the seats were removed and a huge load of stores – not all ours! – loaded. Finally, two seats were replaced. It all seemed so casual. I felt distinctly uneasy!

Around 8.30 am we left Dum Dum, a mere two and a half hours late. If only we had known, we could have started the day at a more reasonable, though much hotter hour.

The breakfast provided was a stone cold omelette: this I ate and Anna's too. Heaven knows what organisms were lurking in it, for I was desperately ill for 24 hours with the most awful diarrhoea and vomiting I have ever suffered. I resolved there and then never to touch food on a Nepalese flight!

Normally, as one flies due north from Calcutta to the little airport on the Indo-Nepalese border, the gigantic Himalayan mountain range can be clearly seen, but this was mid April; there had been no proper rains since October, the ground was burnt and parched. Dust in the air severely limited the view.

The captain landed the rickety old Dakota on a "grass" strip as smoothly as if on tarmac. These pilots are first class, they have to be! The radio station had long since broken down, they flew by map reading.

It was difficult to believe that there were any officials for no one wore uniform. The custom formalities were cut short by Jim who immediately volunteered that I had nothing to declare – he was desperately anxious to get back to Dharan. He was leaving the following day. Stunned by this declaration, I did however voice that my luggage contained a tape recorder. I could hardly have done other, as it was only wrapped in polythene and stood three feet away! "You must take it to our Head Office," said the officer. "No, we won't," replied my colleague, for he suspected that the official just wanted a lift into town! Much haggling and squabbling took place. I stood back, an embarrassed bystander, though the centre of the furore. It was now 10.30 am and getting uncomfortably hot for Anna and the baby. Finally a compromise was agreed and I signed various papers and the tape recorder came with me; it was a very good thing that I left the negotiating to Jim, as I later discovered, once I had given it up, I would never have seen it again.

Meanwhile, I was taking stock of the surroundings – hard baked earth, suffocating heat, a sea of black umbrellas. Just what had I brought Anna and the baby to? Why had I volunteered for such a posting when I could have gone to Cyprus, Hong Kong or Singapore? I felt very depressed.

The landrover, with our luggage filling the accompanying trailer, was soon cruising along the thirty mile, single track road, to Dharan. The heat became less oppressive. We sped past Hindu and Buddhist temples, bullock carts and water buffalo, crude rickshaws and decrepit lorries. The further we progressed, the greener the grass appeared. There is a water shelf just below.

A little girl darted across the road in front of us. The driver stood on the brakes and we lurched to a sickening stop. Then we noticed a little group of children: they were playing "dare". The driver swore solidly at the child for at least two minutes. If he had hit her, he would automatically have been thrown into gaol. We continued our journey, passing through little villages, where dogs were basking in the sun on the hot tarmac and most reluctant to move, even to repeated honking of the horn.

My morale rose when, quite unexpectedly, we entered deep forest. The sal trees were enormous, huge creepers hung down from the branches. It was so peaceful and clean. My eyes were skinned for animals but all we were to see was a family of monkeys playing on the road. We continued for eight miles through the jungle, which extends right across Nepal, before turning briefly along the top edge to the cantonment, that had been built three to four miles from the foothills of the Himalayas.

I was agreeably surprised by the excellent state of the road during our drive; there were no potholes and the sides were in near perfect condition. I later learned that the road, constructed by the Royal Engineers, was constantly maintained by a road gang of forty men, at an annual cost of £20.000. Most work is done to the culverts, as these are badly damaged every monsoon. By now we could make out, through the haze, the outline of the hills, that were to afford such pleasure in the next two years. The cantonment was entirely different to what I had imagined, not a collection of buildings on a ploughed field, but an oasis of order and cleanliness.

It was a village of bungalows with immaculate roads, lined by flame trees. Though the grass was brown and burnt, the flowering shrubs had not suffered from the drought. A row of jacaranda stood below the hospital, their blue flowers contrasting beautifully with the orange of the flame trees. As we approached our future home, the drive led to where red bougainvillaea cascaded over the roof of the porch to the bungalow standing in half an acre of garden. A few tomatoes, lettuces and cauliflowers still survived the heat and dryness, thanks to constant attention of the mali (gardener), Narbahadur. In addition there were banana and pawpaw trees.

There were three bedrooms with a small air conditioner in the en-suite, a second bathroom, while a corridor ran the whole length of the building. Large fans were set in the ceilings. An enormous living-room, with a wooden screen, that could divide the room, filled the centre of the bungalow and boasted a huge fireplace! Anna was delighted with the spacious kitchen. A verandah extended along the back, ideal for packing, unpacking and storing crates. Round the whole bungalow were deep monsoon drains.

In the back garden was a little patio, a tiny paddling pool and a swing. With this luxurious home came the cook, Dawa, (earning £11 per month), the bearer, Kharkabahadur (£8), the ayah, Doma (£8) and the mali, Narbahadur (£7). My salary, for working with the Gurkhas, was excellent compared with what we earned in England. Everything seemed perfect, yet within three months we had dismissed both cook and bearer! Their irritating habits far outweighed their usefulness. Our predecessor had twelve bearers during his tour and Kharkabahadur was proud to be the thirteenth. We were uncomfortable having servants standing by the wall as we ate and had to be constantly reminded not to start hoovering at daybreak, whilst we were asleep.

OUR BUNGALOW, THE WATER TOWER BEYOND

The cook, (the senior servant and most highly paid,) often would not carry out tasks Anna set him. She enquired of the ayah why this was so and Doma explained that he did not take orders from a woman. Anna warned Dawa that, whilst her husband was at work, she was his mouthpiece and he must do as she requested or leave. On that occasion he did finally defrost the fridge but soon became awkward. We were frustrated to find, every evening, our omelettes ready cooked at exactly the same time, before we had even left the golf course, the result being that they were always cold. In exasperation we fired him and Anna did the cooking. Her very first task was to request the quartermaster to fit mesh covers to the kitchen windows. As a result, almost immediately, our bowel habits became normal and it was only when dining out that we were "loose" next day. We were soon to be too hectic at the hospital to play much golf.

As the bearer had been sacked and his jobs included cleaning, we employed Doma's younger sister Kanche and Naumati, who had been a patient on the Families ward. Naumati polished and the Brigadier commented on the glass like sheen to our floor, assuming it was due to the efforts of the bearer. An irritating side to Naumati was her body odour and she brought her baby, who always seemed to have a cold. He was propped up on the sofa whilst she worked. Anna gave her baby clothes, that were surplus to her needs, with the result that Naumati dressed her's in three layers of cardigans; in 100°F (38°C) this was unwise. Anna provided her with soap but she still smelled, as she sold this in the market! Kanche and Doma cared for the babies, laundering and washing up, which we stacked after lunch and supper and were happy working together. Anna knew that on our return home she would have house, garden and children to cope with, so was glad to do something other than ride, swim, play tennis and golf; though the opportunity to read every book in the cantonment library, that appealed to her, was wonderful. If a book was really gripping she could read literally all day.

Among the British Gurkha families, was an unwritten rule not to sack a member of the Rai or Limbu tribes, favoured for joining the Brigade of Gurkhas. When we left, Narbahadur was immediately employed by the Gurkha officer living opposite. Incidentally, as the recruits were taught their drill, the instructors shouted "Limbu, Rai! Limbu, Rai! Limbu, Rai!" instead of "Left, Right! Left, Right! Left, Right!".

Doma, the ayah, considered "the best in the camp", had a little home opposite the kitchen door. When we learned that the next incumbent had no children and would not need her, Anna worried that she would lose her abode and therefore her son his schooling. Anna offered to show her how to wait at table but she was not interested.

The terrace was my favourite location in the evenings, especially when Ronald Bryan, Bishop of Barrackpore, came to visit us, which he did every six months. There we would sit, gin and tonic in hand, gazing into the star studded sky, watching the satellites shudder their course in an arc above us. He was really Bishop of Calcutta. Ronald baptised our daughter, Rachel, born September 6th 1967, on a bi-annual visit, in Dharan cantonment church on December 27th 1967. Years later we were to visit St Peter's Church, Ardleigh Green Road, Hornchurch, where his plaque was on the wall.

DOMA WITH JAMES

This is to certify that Rachael Louise
the daughter of Peter and Anna Pitts
was baptized by me in Dhanan
cantonment Church of the 27th
December 1967.

+Ronald Bryan

Bishop of Banackpore

BACKGROUND

Cooking the evening meal, when so many accidents occur.

CHAPTER 7

Nepal

A heavily tattooed Tharu woman.

Nepal extends five hundred and twenty miles east to west, yet only from eighty-nine to one-hundred-and-fifty north to south. The land mass is similar to England and Northern Ireland combined. This land-locked country lies to the North

East of India, which also extends to cover the West. Tibet occupies the North, but in name only, it is China in reality. The ground to the South is flat, an extension of the northern plains of India. This is the terai and it is in the northerly parts that the dense jungle is situated.

Two fifths of the country is covered with forest and shrub land with a further fifth, the Midland Hills, under cultivation. In the tropical lowland rain forest are sal trees with rhododendron, oak and conifer up to the timberline at about 12,000 feet, while dwarf alpine scrubs and grasslands may survive to perhaps 20,000 feet.

There are 175 species of mammals, 847 of birds, 180 of fresh water fish, 640 of butterflies, 80 of reptiles, and 4440 of insects. There are 7000 species of flowering plants. 800 plants are used for medicine, of which 50 are commercially exported.

The terai was once only populated by the heavily tattooed Tharu tribe. They alone could withstand malaria. It was because of the anophyles mosquito, that this was once, for others, one of the most deadly places in the world to live. Now the World Health Organisation, has practically eradicated malaria from Nepal. From the terai, rise up the foothills to the Himalayas. In the centre and further west, the ground rises more gently and low sand hills called siwaliks are present. There are two areas of inner terai. In the centre is Chitaman, here the Rapti river flows and King Mahendra established his thousand square mile game reserve, where "Tiger Tops" is situated. The other is Dang where the Babai flows. Both are surrounded by mountains. Further north is a mountain range, with the peaks 6-7000 feet, extending across Nepal and called the Mahabharat Lekh.

The most important part of Nepal, (as far as finding soldiers is concerned,) is the Midland Hills, 1500 to 5000 feet, with the valley of Kathmandu (4500 feet) and Pokhara (2000 feet) the best known areas. Here the majority of the population of 10 million live and where recruiters seek young men from Rais, Gurungs, Magars, Limbus, Sunwars, Tamangs and Puns for the British Army. These tribes produce natural fighters.

From here, the mountain ranges rise steadily higher to the great peaks: Mount Everest, Kanchejunga, Makalu, Annapurna and Machhapuchhare. 15% of Nepal is under permanent snow, with over 200 mountains with an elevation in excess of 21,000 feet.

The main towns are Biratnager and Dharan to the east, (the industrial area), Bhairawa in the centre, adjacent to Paklihawa, the western recruiting station, and Nepalganj in the west. Rice, jute, wheat, sugar cane and mustard oil grow plenteously in the terai and are important exports. (Jute and sugar to China and timber, raw jute and wool to the Soviet Union.)

Cutting through the huge mountain masses are great rivers: the Kosi near Dharan, the Bagmati (sacred as it runs into the most sacred Ganges) arising from the Kathmandu valley, the Narayani in the middle and the Seti, Karnali, Bheri and Babai in the west. These divide Nepal so completely that, in the rainy season, it may be quite impossible to cross them. For this reason the majority of roads, such as the British Biratnager-Dharan and the Indian 125 mile Tribhuvan Rajpath – the principal road to Kathmandu from Raxaul in India and Birgang in Nepal – are all north-south. Before this, anything needed in Kathmandu had to be manhandled over the mountains. This included such items as Rolls Royces for the Rana rulers, and a grand piano. Already there is a sad difference in the roads. The Indians handed over upkeep of the Rajpath to the Nepalese in 1966. The road has sadly deteriorated, a tragedy, considering the highly skilled performance in cutting such a passage through the mountains.

The Chinese have completed their 100 mile road from Tibet to Kathmandu, an ominous sign of the not too distant future, I suspect, for the road has been built wide and strong enough to take tanks. Now the accent is on a east-west highway, being started by Indian, American and British engineers during the time I was there (1966-1968.) It is a tremendous undertaking, having to cross many huge rivers, but once completed, the whole country will open up.

CHAPTER 8

The British Military Hospital

After the partition of India in 1947, British establishments were opened at Katakpahur, Kunraghat, ("ghat" means "landing stage",) and Calcutta; these were moved later to Jalapahar, Lehra and Barrackpore, the latter virtually a suburb of Calcutta.

The British Gurkha recruitment depôt at Lehra had a forty bedded camp hospital, later replaced by thatched brick huts. This tented camp had a similar set up to the British Military Hospital in Dharan. There were four male, a female and a one bedded maternity ward! There was an operating theatre, a medical stores-cum-dispensary, medical inspection (MI) room, and an isolation wing, which could number up to seven outdoor tents. Two doctors ran the hospital, with the help of a midwife and female ward assistant. There was one Gurkha State Registered Nurse, five ex-R.A.M.C. Anglo-Indian nursing orderlies, and the MI room orderly. Ranjit Rai, the administrative officer of the British Military Hospital, joined the hospital at Lehra as a nursing orderly in 1952, when huts had been built and electricity installed. Previously, during night duty, the nursing orderlies had to visit the various tented wards with the aid of a hurricane-lamp. Lehra was alive with snakes, so that every step was precarious; the wisest way to progress, even with a hurricane-lamp, was to strike the ground with a stick before each step; this set up vibrations to frighten most snakes away.

During the time the hospital was at Lehra, first Birbhusan Thapa and later Udai Sing Subba joined the hospital as nursing orderlies. Over the years these three men have all been promoted and hold key posts in administration, reception and the male ward. The latter two have recently been awarded their "three stripes".

I am very glad I never had to work in Lehra. The camp was situated a three hour drive by landrover, south west of Paklihawa. This is in the northern plains of India where it is incredibly hot, just as it is in Calcutta. In the days of the British Raj, there was a mass exodus to the hill stations, including Darjeeling and Simla, at the end of April and beginning of May. The temperature in the shade in Lehra was 116 - 118°F (in excess of 45°C), whereas, even in the hot season in Dharan, it only reached this in the sun and rarely made more than 100 °F (38°C) in the shade.

Apart from the snakes (mostly cobra) were other hazards, including scorpion stings, which occurred frequently so that the reception staff became adept in dealing with them, that a doctor was never called. Scorpions certainly exist in Dharan, but I neither saw one nor dealt with their sting in my two year tour, though Jill Garwood, our next door neighbour, found one under the bathmat! Scorpions are about three and a half inches long and are most commonly found by the sides of rivers in rotten wood. They are one reason why the village houses are built on stilts.

In my African experience, scorpion stings, though not lethal, are agonisingly painful so that even morphia has little effect in neutralising the pain. The treatment is, however, so simple and effective that it is a pity people have to suffer pain for long. All one has to do, is to inject a little local anaesthetic into the region of the sting and the pain disappears at once. These days there is a long acting local anaesthetic, bupivicaine, effective for up to 18 hours, ideal in the management of such pain.

Cyclones were another hazard. They seemed to blow every six months or so. They also occur in Dharan when one cut a broad swathe through the forest, tearing through the graveyard, before continuing down the golf course, where several of my most hated trees were uprooted. These were the obstacles I would invariably hit as I sliced and hooked my way down the fairway! Nearly every garden lost at least one tree that night.

Finally, in the pre-monsoon period of March to June, hot sandstorms called "Loo" winds spring up most days and blow from 10.00 am till midnight, making life particularly oppressive (the "scratchy" season).

It was in Lehra that Ranjit learned to administer anaesthetics. From his tales, I feel that he is a great deal happier with administrative work than he ever was with the "rag and bottle"! For a very long time the hospital never had a senior anaesthetist; general duty medical officers learned to give anaesthetics "the hard way". It was not in fact till 1963 that a specialist anaesthetist (Geoff O'Connell) was posted to Dharan. Several junior surgeons had been sent to Nepal but the first Fellow of the Royal College of Surgeons was Major Gulati, also in 1963. Yet at this little hospital, more major surgery was performed than at practically any other military establishment in the British Armed Forces.

Meanwhile in 1957, a Medical Reception Station was set up for the cantonment construction camp at Phusre, which is about three miles due north of the present camp at Dharan. This is a lovely location, tucked in much closer to the foothills. It is several hundred feet higher than the present camp and correspondingly cooler. However there were drawbacks for, though sufficient room for us, there was insufficient flat land to build a camp anything like the present size.

In March 1959, the British Military Hospital moved out of India to Paklihawa in Western Nepal. By now the entire hospital nursing staff were Nepalese. Two other great personalities joined, Hirabahadur Pun to assist Udai Sing in reception and Harkabahadur Subba, affectionately known as "HB", the dispenser. I found him one of the most helpful members of the staff. He quickly learned to decipher my handwriting.

The hospital was established at its present site, two miles from the town and thirty miles of the border. There was limitless flatland. The first ward of the present hospital opened on October 2nd 1960 and the story of the British Military Hospital in Dharan began.

A <u>dharan</u> – wood cutting frame.

At that time, there was a lot of political unrest in the bazaar and Nepal generally. Kathmandu (the capital), Biratnager and Dharan were the main centres of Communist activity. Finally, King Mahendra banned all political parties but not before "the hammer and sickle" had been seen flying from many houses in Dharan. It was because of this that uniformed troops were banned from entering the bazaar (township), with subsequent difficulties over supplies. The other reason the camp had to be moved was the tripartite agreement between Great Britain, Nepal and India for the establishment of any Gurkha recruiting depot in Nepal: that any camp had to be stationed no more than thirty miles from the Indian border.

"Dharan" means the frame used for wood sawing, that being the main local industry. A frame is erected at head height. A two man saw is used to cut the trunk, which is fixed horizontally on top of the frame. Usually one man, standing on top, holds the saw while a second stands below to control the direction, with the aid of a plumb-line, resulting in very accurate and rapid delivery. There are many variations to the "dharan"; for example, the lower man is sometimes standing in a pit. When I first saw the cutting in action, at a distance, I noticed how the second drew the saw right down between his legs. I imagined what awful accidents might follow until I realised that the blade was actually facing away from his vital parts!

In 1958 the forest extended right up to the foot-hills. An extensive area of forest had first to be cleared to build the cantonment. Many were the vast sal (shorea robusta) trees, whose timber must be worked while green, as it soon becomes very hard. Carpenters tell me that it is then difficult even to bang a nail into it, so that drilling may be necessary. The felled timber was rapidly utilised in the construction of the camp.

Although the British Government had bought the land from the Nepalese Government, the locals resisted the sale, as they still do land reforms brought in by the Government. The people scarcely recognised that there was a government in Kathmandu!

45

One problem the tree fellers came across was cutting the sacred trees, to which the villagers strongly protested. Some were preserved but others still had to be bulldozed.

Communications are vital. It used to take twenty four hours to travel along the laterite (clay) track between Biratnager and Dharan and then only if by horse, before the tarmac road. These thirty miles of road took three years to construct at a cost of between £500,000 and £700,000.

The project commenced in 1956 and followed the old bullock track due north of Jogbani. A bridge had to be built over the Dhubi river; this was a major problem for there was literally nothing in the way of mechanical aid in Nepal. Bulldozers and rollers had to be shipped from Singapore to Calcutta, with the various hold-ups and frustrations that seem inevitable in India. From Calcutta these were taken to the Ganges, on broad gauge railway, shipped over the water on barges and then loaded on to narrow gauge, finally to reach Jogbani – with at least part of the consignment that had been originally loaded at the Singapore docks! Once a case of champagne was ordered. Only one bottle survived, making its cost prohibitive so no one bought it; out of a box of 24 tins of beer, one made it.

We could hear the roar of the approach of the monsoon – like a train going through a tunnel. The downpour caused considerable damage, but it is the bridges and culverts that take the main brunt of the deluge, a trickling stream converted into a raging torrent in a few moments. An engineering friend described how he witnessed a wall of water racing towards him, while standing on a bridge, yet at that precise moment the river-bed below was bone dry.

Falling off a bullock cart.

Water is not the only hazard. On each side of the tarmac strip is six feet of beaten earth, from where the sides of the road fall sharply into huge ditches, full of water in the monsoon. The Tharus use these to soak their jute. The mills are at Biratnager. The beaten earth road was built for the main traffic: bullock and buffalo carts. These have home-made wooden wheels, often reinforced by a metal rim. The effect on the tarmac, especially with the cart loaded high with timber, is cruel. They are not permitted on the hard surface, but what is legal and what is actually done are very different things in Nepal! Broken-down trucks are another hazard. This is sometimes a burst tyre in the more "modern" vehicle; the wheel has been removed and a heap of stones placed as a jack for support, while the driver may have hitched a lift to town.

As often as not, the carts are found in the middle of the road – one reason being that the driver is fast asleep, when the bullocks, naturally, choose the most comfortable surface! The somniferous habit of the drivers caused me problems for, too often, they fell out of their carts. It could be quite a considerable drop from a loaded cart. The wheels were an additional hazard. I had to deal with crush injuries resulting from running over a bare foot. The driver had got down to adjust the load, only for the bullocks to start off, with this very painful consequence. Night is the worst time to encounter vehicles, for however hard one blows the horn, the drivers will not budge, being soundly asleep. Indeed it was not only moving obstacles that we met. Sometimes they had been deliberately stopped, the bullocks untied, the cart turned on its end, for shelter, and the driver asleep, all bang in the middle of the road.

At one time, when the presence of these carts had become a complete menace, the Anglo-Indian in charge of the road gang used to remove the wooden peg to the yoke so that the animals could no longer pull the cart. The peg would then be deposited at the police station, which might be anything from two to thirty miles away. To get it back, he would have to walk or hitch a lift and possibly pay a fine. More often the road gang leader would simply hurl it as far as possible into the forest, cursing: "Get off the tarmac!" In the quagmire of the monsoon, it might take a considerable time to recover.

I am told of a particularly mischievous engineer, finding a bullock cart in the middle of the road with the driver asleep, stealthily turned the bullocks round before giving an encouraging kick! There was much speculation as to how far they got before the driver woke.

The Nepalese Government were quick to cash in; they made it a toll road and at one time even expected, or at least hoped, that the drivers of British vehicles would also pay!

No one at the camp had his own personal vehicle, nor was any British soldier allowed to drive, apart from the warrant officer in charge of transport. Even he was confined to within five miles of the camp and then only when road testing. The rule was made for the safety of the British, for the repercussions for harming a pedestrian or sacred cow, whoever's fault it is, can be very severe. The driver, as in Calcutta, is in danger of lynching by the crowd, which will appear as if from nowhere.

I had been at Nepal six months before I dealt with my first road traffic accident. An Indian student had been crushed by a three-ton lorry which was backing against a wall. Even that incident occurred inside the cantonment and the student had been trespassing anyway!

A major incident did finally occur. It was a disaster. Reception was full of bodies, with blood everywhere. The Nepalese police, stationed at Dharan, had had an urgent call to get to Biratnager because of student rioting. News had filtered through that, two weeks earlier, there had been trouble in Kathmandu when a policeman had been "too rough" with students. The agitators were now rioting in sympathy! Seventeen policemen crammed into a Russian jeep and were tearing down the middle of the road. A lorry was approaching from the opposite direction. The drivers of both vehicles blasted their horns. As usual, neither took a blind bit of notice. Neither would give way, the police expecting the lorry to, they being the police, the lorry expected the police to, theirs being the smaller vehicle. At the last second, the jeep was forced to swerve to avoid a head on collision. It rolled over several times, killing two inspectors sharing the front seat. The driver was fortunate to escape with a fractured pelvis. Of the fourteen in the back, one died immediately, but the rest survived. Apart from one serious head injury, they mostly escaped with cuts and bruises and were all out of hospital within a month.

Resistance to the hospital and the cantonment persisted in the early years. Vehicles were stoned in the bazaar and there were unpleasant incidents when leaflets were strewn in the road, accusing the British of employing Nepalese nurses for immoral purposes. Some of the agitators came from the Indian hill station of Darjeeling, fifty miles as the crow flies, but a day's journey by train. It was in Darjeeling that Chinese indoctrinated students.

While I was there all appeared peaceful. In these seven years the population has increased tenfold, from approximately one to ten thousand, with four times this number in the surrounding area.

At least a thousand are employed in the cantonment. These have an army of dependants. One of the most endearing characteristics of the Nepalese is loyalty to their families, especially their parents. A very large percentage of their meagre pay is spent thus, to them perfectly natural, not even considered as generosity. The hill people work very hard to make a living yet, by the end of the year, they have little to show for it. The average labourer's wage in the cantonment is about 150 rupees. This is a little under £8 per month. The nursing orderlies in the hospital earn up to £25 a month, while some wages reach a staggering £50. This far exceeds anything the Nepalese can earn in the hills. The standard diet is rice supplemented by vegetables, very little meat is eaten. Less is spent on clothing and the houses are mostly hand built. Practically no luxury goods are bought so there is little need for money. The odd pice (100 pice make 1 rupee, 1 rupee = 5p) is spent on <u>bidis</u>, (locally made cigarettes). In a country where money and employment are so hard to come by, an institution which offers both is very welcome. In addition the hospital provides a free health service, a unique luxury. This is why the Dharan population is no longer antagonistic towards the British. Even so, we never felt completely at ease walking alone through the town.

Once a child pushed in front of Anna as she was choosing fruit. I took him firmly by the shoulders and lifted him out of the way. As I did so, one of his feet caught in the ropes of the basket containing tangerines and he lay sprawled on the ground. I hurriedly picked him up, in case I had inadvertently caused an incident. Fortunately I was recognised as "Doctor Sahib". The event was ignored.

It is difficult to know why the camp was ever located at Dharan, in the extreme East, many miles from the main recruiting areas, thirty miles from the nearest railway, with no telephonic communications or even water!

It was in fact water that had decided the site. The Royal Engineers, through a brilliant feat of engineering, built a pipeline from high in the hills, where a river is flowing constantly all year round. The pipeline feeds a water-tank that contains 100,000 gallons of water. Here the water is filtered and chlorinated so tap water is safe to drink. The cantonment must be one of the few places in the sub-continent where one can safely drink water from the tap.

The four features which impress American guests from Kathmandu are the cleanliness, the street lights, the curbs and the drinking water.

The tower, built on huge cement stilts, reaches a height of nearly a hundred feet. It is virtually the heart of the cantonment for if destroyed, or the water polluted, life in the cantonment would be difficult. It is cool underneath, so a popular meeting place, especially for private servants, (normally off duty from 2.30pm to 5.30pm), in the hottest months of April, May and June. Two popular games were, flicking a small pebble to land as close as possible to a marker some fifteen paces in front, and knocking a three-inch piece of wood up into the air and then striking it as far as possible with a longer stick. However, they soon tired of this and got down to gambling, strictly forbidden in Nepal. It was my bearer who was caught by the senior Gurkha officer – the Gurkha Major – who turned out to be the organising brain. These activities ceased forthwith!

Wasps and bees, as well as bearers, were attracted to the water-tower, for the walls were cool, high, and did not sway in the breeze. Huge nests were built high up the supports to the tower which the hygiene squad had to destroy. This was done when just dark, usually at dusk. The practice was to send a note to each residence to warn what was to happen, so that the windows and doors could be closed to prevent angry insects, attracted by light, from entering the home.

It was the postman's job to deliver this notice and also the mail. The post arrived most evenings between 6.00pm and 7.00pm and to save an extra journey, the postman delivered the notices, irrespective of their importance, at the same time! He had no idea what they contained as he could neither speak nor read English; (the names on the envelopes were re-written in Gurkhali,) otherwise, on these dangerous occasions, he might have hurried for his own safety!

When this first happened, I had returned from the hospital, soon after 6.00pm, to be greeted by Anna, who was reading the cantonment orders, with "What time is 18.00 hours?" Even as I had entered, two angry wasps had come in with me! We rushed round closing windows and slamming doors; finally I was left with six to deal with while Anna made a rapid retreat into her safe kitchen.

Another advantage of the water-tower was its value as a landmark. The ground to the foothills is flat and featureless, so the tower can be spotted from a distance – a welcome sight after a long trek (or even a short one in the heat!)

There are two occasions in the year when water supplies may be restricted, though never on anything like the scale in Hong Kong where, in July, they were limited to four hours every four days. Ironically, one of these is the worst of the monsoon. At this time the water is beautifully soft, being virtually rain water. I first noticed this when 'scrubbing up' for an operation. The drain below was bubbling up like a sink full of detergent.

Because of the rains, landslides occur and these can bend or break the pipe; in addition a lot of earth enters the supply, silting and partially blocking it. It can take hours digging to locate the pipe and longer the site of blockage. We had the ludicrous situation of water pouring down all round yet a warning to cut its use to a minimum.

The other time is, naturally enough, in the hottest season of April – June before the monsoon breaks. This is a time when one of the extraordinary weaknesses of the Nepalese becomes apparent. All their lives they have lived with the problem of water and the dire consequences of shortage, yet, in spite of repeated requests to economise, they simply allow taps to run so that, even at night, thousands of gallons are wasted. This loss became so serious that the supply to the Gurkha lines had to be cut off during sleeping hours.

CHAPTER 9

Earthquake

Nepal is a potential earthquake area and thirty years eatlier a whole street in Kathmandu was destroyed. For this reason, mostly bungalow-type buildings were erected with the architects avoiding too much masonry above; the hope being that if an earthquake did occur, the damage need not be too catastrophic. *(Twenty years after I had left, an earthquake was to destroy the whole town of Dharan (see epilogue)).*

The evidence of an earthquake was forcibly brought to my attention when I saw Tilakbahadur's face, as we passed one afternoon in the corridor outside the maternity ward. There was

A young man, after cutting grass on the hospital grounds.

a scar that extended from his right temple, at the hair-line, right across his forehead through his left eyebrow, eyelid and eye, to disappear across his face. I presumed that his wound had been sutured for it had healed soundly, but I couldn't understand how any doctor could have left the eyelid in such a mess, resulting in practically the complete loss of sight. He could only distinguish light. I was so intrigued that I suggested he might come to my Out Patients, not realising at the time I was to see sixty-three that afternoon before his turn came! He was in hospital because I had just performed an emergency Caesarian on his wife, and had delivered a lovely little girl. (Sadly girls are not very popular at the best of times, for one day the father will have to provide a dowry; to have undergo a Caesarian for a baby girl was to add insult to injury!)

Tilakbahadur was a tailor and had lived most of his life in Bhojpur until recently coming to live in Dharan. This is five days walk and Tilakbahadur's terrible scars had been inflicted thirty-eight years earlier when only ten years old. One ill-fated morning, he had got up at dawn to cut grass near the jungle. At midday he was staggering home with a large sack on his back, taking the weight on his forehead with a headband. He was halfway along a steep narrow path leading to his village when the earthquake struck. A rock was dislodged from the mountain to crash on to his head, splitting it open as if it were a coconut. That was all Tilakbahadur could remember. For twenty-two days he hovered between life and death. He was fed by his family with buffalo milk pushed into his mouth with a spoon. It took two years for his head to heal and he had never seen a doctor until now. Only one man had been killed in his village but many houses were destroyed. Six miles away at Shamshila, a hundred had perished. Tilakbahadur's eye was red and painful and looked quite disgusting. I offered to try to reconstruct his eyelid, remove his eye and put in a glass one, which we could get for fifty pence. He refused. If I couldn't restore his sight, he didn't want anything. No, not even an upper eyelid with which he could cover his bad eye? If he could live all this time with his eye like this, he would leave things alone! I did however feel more sorry for his wife and daughter, for they had to look at this horrible sight.

However, while an earthquake was a possibility, the monsoons are a fact and asphalt roofing and tar has to be added to all buildings in an attempt to prevent leaking roofs, which still occurred in spite of every effort.

Thousands of gallons of water pour down the deep monsoon drains into the forest below, where an experimental farm has been built to teach retiring Gurkha soldiers modern ideas on farming. This is only one of the resettlement projects in the camp.

The Kukri maker at night. These are some 20 inches long and, in the leather sheath, is a short knife - the <u>karda</u> and a third blunt blade, a <u>chakmak</u>, to start fires.

Lesser drains are built round all the buildings and these feed into the main drains, which caused me work as children fell into them, cutting their faces and breaking their limbs. I have also had to repair the wounds of inebriated adults who have stumbled into them in search of home.

The cantonment was really like a little town. There are three schools, a church which is shared by the British school children, a temple for the Nepalese, a sewage farm, a large store and a collection of little shops including a tailor, a photographer, a barber, a goldsmith, a watch repair shop, a Bata shoe shop, a cobbler, a bakery and a little restaurant offering wild boar or chicken curry.

I found the kukri maker the most interesting to visit, especially in the cool of the evening. He used the best quality steel: the springs from a written–off army landrover. It is fascinating to watch the kukri being beaten into shape by powerful blows of a huge hammer on the red hot metal.

I never liked to get too close, as sparks shot off in every direction, yet the blacksmith never wore goggles. An accident did occur but not what I expected. The huge hammer head flew off as it struck the metal and hit the man (whose job it was working the bellows, to keep the charcoal as hot as possible) violently on the chest. He was most fortunate to escape with a fractured sternum (breast bone) but it was several weeks before he could take a deep breath or clear his throat without stabbing pain.

The most ironical title of the British Gurkha 'L of C' is its name: "Lines of Communication". We did not even have telephonic communication with the airstrip at Biratnager. The main link with Calcutta was by two couriers who left Dharan on Tuesdays and Fridays to take the train the grim 24 hour journey to Barrackpore. I soon learnt that the only realistic way to communicate with the outside world was by these men.

I received two cables from England during my posting. The first took seven days and ended "letter to follow", which arrived three days before! The cable had arrived in Kathmandu within 24 hours, only to take six days to reach Dharan, some 150 miles. The second took a mere five days to arrive! During my last month, B.O.A.C sent a telegram from Calcutta to say my plane would leave two hours earlier, because of the new summer schedule beginning on April 1st. It took twelve days to reach me.

Another example of lack of communications was over air transport. During the monsoon season, the Biratnager grass air-strip is too muddy for planes to land. This means that for three months, the only way in and out of Dharan is by road and rail. It was for this reason that we have to be prepared to tackle a surgical emergency in any specialty.

At least this lack of air transport did worry the authorities and an all-weather airfield was constructed, with Indian aid, three miles closer to Dharan. This was completed well before the monsoon broke in June 1967. Now there seemed to be no problem about air lifts; vital supplies could arrive by Beverley (plane) from Singapore and no longer would there be frustrating delays for medical and other vital equipment for the cantonment. To mention just one: when I arrived the supply of size 7 surgical operating gloves was very limited. If I wore size 6½ my hands felt cramped during a long operation and if I wore 7½ I would have to push the excess down each finger. We requested several hundred pairs. They arrived from Singapore... one year after our urgent signal... all had perished! These delays occur in the docks of Calcutta where I heard hair-raising stories of chaos and corruption. With the new all-weather strip, there should be no problem for the Gurkha soldier and his family. He could be in Singapore or Hong Kong and return to Dharan in a matter of hours.

But of course snags developed! The Nepalese either would not or could not run the airfield. It was rumoured that they had not budgeted for, or would not buy, the requisite electrical fittings. Soon grass was pushing up between the concrete slabs; either not enough top soil had been removed or insufficient weed killer put down. The airfield was to lie unused, a huge white elephant!

One nagging worry I had was what we should do if the Chinese came. We were not allowed firearms, being simply a recruiting depot, and could only muster an armoury of nine shot-guns. All the Chinese would have to do, was land a plane on the golf course, adjacent to the camp, and the cantonment would be theirs. In the monsoon, they would only have to drop a few paratroops. This could so easily happen yet no one in the outside world might ever know, so bad are the communications!

The hospital had about seventy beds. One ward, named the Gurkha Other Rank, (G.O.R.), was divided by Sister's office, lavatories, baths and kitchens into two, each of fourteen beds, one medical, the other surgical. There are two air-conditioned side wards which were used for desperately ill patients. We also used these for our British Non Commissioned Officers (N.C.Os) and their families, together with American Pearce Corps volunteers who often came for attention, as they lived in the villages.

A tuberculosis (TB) unit is separate from the male ward and divided into two, positive and negative. In the infectious stage of TB, live bacteria are present in the sputum which is highly infectious. TB is spread, like the common cold, by coughs and sneezes. The infected sputum can be examined, by microscope, on a glass slide, after it has been specifically prepared with the Ziehl-Nielsen stain.

Frequently we send sputum or pus for examination for "A.A.F.B". This means TB but, not wanting to frighten the patient, when the disease is suspected but not confirmed, we use this term. It means "acid and alcohol fast bacillus" and TB is the only bacteria which has these characteristics. Even that is too long so the shorter term of "A.F.B" (acid fast bacillus) is used.

Some weeks after commencement of triple therapy, which means giving three standard anti-TB drugs – Streptomycin, (by injection), Para-Aminosalicylic Acid (PAS) and Isoniazid (INAH), the sputum should no longer contain these bacilli. When the patients are no longer infectious, they are transferred from the positive to the negative ward, until they have completed three months of injections. They should continue on the tablets for a further fifteen to twenty four months, though few actually do, resulting in drug resistance.

Families ward had nine adult beds and six cots, though the latter had to be increased dramatically at times and little wicker baskets were ideal for young babies. Jim Arnott donated his old pram and this provided a perfectly suitable cot on more than one occasion. A small air-conditioned sideward off the Families ward was kept for British families. The little midwifery unit consisted of three beds, as well as a first stage unit, a delivery room and a tiny nursery with incubator. The Officers ward was hardly ever used, so became a recovery ward following out-patient surgery, a room for taking blood and an alternative theatre. The Central Sterile Supply Depot (CSSD) was near by, plus the medical library. The remainder of the hospital consisted of reception, consulting and treatment rooms; the latter two were air-conditioned during my second year, vastly improving our comfort and efficiency. The dispensary, medical stores, x-ray department, pathology laboratory, theatre, dental centre (used for two weeks, four times a year) and a second out-patient block, (where TB and villagers' clinics were held), completed the hospital, apart from the administration block run by one man: Ranjit Rai.

As I spent most of my time either operating or seeing out-patients, I guess I was the luckiest of three doctors, spending most of my day in air-conditioned rooms! The commanding officer, Major Mike Banahan, (later Major Gordon Sommerville) and the anaesthetist, Major Vincent Noone, to be replaced by Major Jim O'Donnell, completed the trio.

PROBLEMS

A <u>doli</u> – how some patients were carried to hospital.

CHAPTER 10

Mango Tree

The mango season of May to July certainly kept me very busy. At one time I had four little boys in hospital, all with injuries sustained from falling from these trees.

Typical was that of eleven year old Bharat, who had climbed high into such a tree to pick the delicious fruit only for his hand to slip as he reached out for an even higher prize. He crashed straight to the ground without breaking his fall and was brought to hospital the following day, with his hand grotesquely swollen; it had been left to hang limply by his side. He had three fractures: his upper arm (the humerus), his forearm, just below the elbow, and a nasty wrist fracture, a Colles fracture, when the hand ends up the shape of a dinner fork. We placed his arm in a sling, to allow the swelling to settle a little and the next day manipulated the bones.

Tears were streaming down his little face as he told me his story. His head was completely shaven apart from a few long strands at the back called a tupi. He was never happy in hospital because, being of the aborigine Tharu tribe, he couldn't understand Nepalese. The nurses had great difficulty communicating with him. He was only happy when I let him home after five days, but thrilled when I removed the above elbow plaster three weeks later. All the fractures had healed perfectly, and his arm felt as light as a feather.

*   *   *   *   *

Twenty-eight year old Adiklal also belonged to the Tharu tribe. He had been some twelve feet from the ground, hacking off branches with his kukri for firewood. He was actually standing on the same branch that he was striking when it tore away from the trunk behind. He landed heavily on his bottom. The sickening thud drove all the air out of him. He was in agony, not daring to move. His friends found him under the tree; he begged them not to touch him. He lay motionless, moaning and groaning. He had fallen at 4.30 p.m. and by 7 p.m. it was nearly dark. He couldn't stay in the forest all night. His friends collected a bullock cart and lifted him into it, despite his loud protests. All that night and the whole of the following day he remained in terrible pain. He could not pass urine.

The villagers placed him back into the same cart and drove him to the hospital. I couldn't examine Adiklal properly, his bladder was so distended. I passed a catheter and released over three pints of blood-stained urine. The relief was instantaneous. He immediately felt so much better that I was able to examine him properly.

He had signs of a ruptured left kidney: his loin was tender, swollen and bruised. I guessed, however, that it probably was not too severe, as he had already survived forty-eight hours, but immediately I performed an intravenous pyelogram, to demonstrate the internal anatomy of each kidney. As I suspected, the pattern of dye in the left kidney was distorted. Though the kidney had been damaged, it was still functioning well. However he could still bleed at any time. Subsequent attempts to pass urine were excruciatingly painful. He required carbachol to function at all. This acts on the bladder, causing it to contract and hopefully void urine. I prescribed sulphonamides to keep the urine sterile and minimise infection.

After a fortnight, he could at least hobble around with a stick and as he could pass clear urine, we let him home. He left hospital a well nourished, fit-looking man, although in considerable pain and still having a struggle to urinate.

Weeks later he appeared at my out-patients. I could barely recognise him. He was emaciated, running a high fever with no control of bladder or bowels. I was shattered. I admitted him immediately and repeated the x-ray to his back. The new films showed that, in his original fall, he had actually fractured his spine.

There are certain fractures which, when first filmed, cannot readily be seen. These breaks become more evident after some days. A classic example is the scaphoid, a little bone in the wrist, said to be shaped like an early Greek boat. This, when broken, typifies these diagnostic difficulties. An x-ray taken after ten days will often demonstrate a crack, which was almost impossible to see before. For this reason we treat such injuries on a clinical basis, rather than rely on radiography. This means we put the forearm in plaster if we suspect such a fracture.

During this time, one of Adiklal's vertebrae had partially collapsed. This explained why he was in so much pain. His fall must also have concussed his spinal cord resulting in incontinence. On top of all this, in his debilitated state, he had contracted typhoid fever, endemic in Nepal; an epidemic was raging at the time.

He made a complete recovery from the typhoid fever with the help of chloramphenicol and the spinal concussion soon recovered. When I saw him next, some weeks later, he was once more a well nourished and now, at last, a happy man. He had no backache and his spine was fully mobile.

*   *   *   *   *

Kharkabahdur, seventeen, came having fallen from his mango tree eight hours earlier. He had at least broken his fall but in a most horrible way! A branch had gone clean through his calf as he crashed through the tree. Otherwise, though very shaken, he had no other injury.

One of the villagers had performed the gruesome task of pulling out the branch. When I saw the affected limb, muscle was bulging through large holes on each side. I sprayed an antibiotic powder on to his wounds and prescribed penicillin. I ordered an injection of anti-tetanus serum to prevent lockjaw. His leg healed beautifully without being sutured.

*   *   *   *   *

Five year old Rambahadur had been playing under a huge mango tree. The previous night a terrific storm flattened hundreds of trees with many more branches ripped off. Rambahadur had chosen a tree where an enormous branch was swaying precariously. A sudden gust sent it crashing. The little lad was pinned to the ground.

Three hours later he arrived at the hospital, a mass of bruises and scratches. His pulse was rapid. As I examined him, he screamed. He was acutely tender over the right upper abdomen, which he held so tightly a condition termed "board hard rigidity". This meant that he couldn't relax, even if he wished. It suggested that, either he had severe bruising of his abdominal muscles or a ruptured internal organ, probably the liver. I asked the two men with him, to each donate a pint of blood. This they willingly did. Both turned out to be Group B, the little boy was group O, their blood was of no use to Rambahadur, but very welcome for my reserves!

I decided to wait and watch. I set up a dextrose drip so that, if his condition suddenly deteriorated, I could at least immediately give plasma or the blood substitute, dextran, without trying to find a vein in a little boy, in a state of collapse.

The nurse carefully recorded his pulse every fifteen minutes throughout the night. Rambahadur's anxious mother guarded the infusion as if it were her life, making certain that the restless child did not dislodge the cannula. She never slept a wink; she had never been in hospital before, never seen a fan, never been in such close proximity to Europeans, if indeed she had ever seen one, she was terrified her child might die.

By dawn, he was no worse and had even managed to sleep fitfully. I had had to sedate him with Vallergan, a hypnotic, though reluctant to "dope" him, for fear of masking a change that might be occurring; a sudden deterioration could necessitate an immediate operation, regardless of whether blood was available or not.

For two long days we religiously continued this regime. Though better, he still refused food, a sure sign a child is not well. I noticed however that mother was tucking into a huge meal, ending, ironically, with a mango! She was obviously happier.

Another two days passed when, quite suddenly, Rambahadur sat up and asked for his mango! This he consumed with great relish; his internal injuries had healed. A few days later he was home.

CHAPTER 11

Hydatid Cyst

Chandri was the forty-one year old wife of a member of the Gurung tribe. She had five children, aged from fourteen to five. Her Gurkha pensioner husband was now a farmer. He owned rice fields, kept cattle, oxen and goats. Unlike most of the villagers in eastern Nepal, they did not keep a dog and Chandri could not remember ever having one in her house. Their home, in the west, had been built on the ground. It was therefore unlike the stilted houses that I found so intriguing in the villages around Dharan.

Chandri had been ill eighteen long months, ever since she had lost a premature baby. All this time she complained that her whole body ached, and the pain had completely taken away the will to eat. Six months before she was finally to arrive at the hospital, she had a second miscarriage, and following this had lost a great deal of blood. The haemorrhage had continued, though irregularly, for several months, before finally drying up so completely that her periods had ceased. In addition, during the past year, she had noticed a firm swelling in the upper abdomen which had, in the course of the three months, increased dramatically in size. From then on her fever never seemed to abate, as her condition worsened. Something had to be done! When she was admitted to the Medical Reception Station at Paklihawa in western Nepal, she was extremely ill. For three weeks Dr Vishnu puzzled over her, while all his investigations drew a blank. Chandri's condition became even more serious. In desperation and in spite of her condition, the doctor sent her to us. She had to face a two day railway journey across the plains of Northern India. Some how she survived.

When I saw her, I too was puzzled. Her abdomen was the shape of an hour-glass. There was a huge mass in the upper abdomen, and another, though much smaller, that rose from her pelvis. My routine investigations did little to help, apart from confirming that she was ill. A test called the Erythrocyte Sedimentation Rate (ESR) recorded sixty-seven. This simple investigation is invaluable in determining just how ill a patient is. It is performed simply by mixing a little blood, taken from a vein, to some citrate solution, which prevents it clotting. The resulting fluid is then drawn up into a long graduated glass tube and placed in a stand. The number of millimetres the erythrocytes (the red cells) fall in one hour is recorded. The normal range in England would be from one to seven, although in Nepal, where anaemia and disease abound, fifteen appears a better average. The ESR is very high in active tuberculosis, but I knew, from my investigations, that she did not have that. In amoebic hepatitis, when amoebae invade the liver and form an abscess, the level can break all records, falling over one hundred and fifty.

While searching her excreta for these wriggling little amoebae, we found the eggs of round and hook worm. The latter is the commonest cause of anaemia in Nepal. However, in this she shared this infestation with 80 per cent of the population. I allowed her four days to recover from the exhausting journey and treatment of these worms before operating. I guessed that she had a huge cyst in the pancreas, but as I had previously dealt with few, if any, such cysts, I consulted the medical library.

"These are very difficult to remove," I read, "but true cysts can occasionally be shelled out." The next tome I researched recorded that they were too rare to be discussed! Much help that was to me.

71

I performed the laparotomy through a long vertical incision. To my shame, I soon diagnosed the lower of the two lumps – an eighteen week pregnancy! She obviously had an attentive husband and was herself a very fertile lady. The upper mass still presented a diagnostic problem. I established that it was probably not malignant, that is, not cancer, as it was so well encapsulated. *(A cancer, which literally means a "crab", eats its way through the tissues.)*

The capsule was firmly stuck to the left half of her diaphragm and the huge lump was restricting her breathing. It was also adherent to that portion of the large bowel termed the transverse colon, as it lies across the abdomen. There were dense adhesions everywhere. The swelling was huge, far bigger than a football. The wall was white and very thick. I was able to peel the various organs off without much difficulty. I had practically shelled it out when it burst. The diagnosis was now all too apparent. It was the largest hydatid cyst I had ever seen. Pus and daughter cysts poured into the abdominal cavity. This was a disaster. Normally, when removing such a tumour, I place large gauze packs around the base so that, should any fluid escape, it is trapped and soaked up, to minimise further contamination. With Chandri's cyst, regrettably, this policy was just not practical. The swelling was so enormous and the adhesions so dense that the surrounding areas could not be so protected.

The danger of a hydatid cyst bursting is twofold. The fluid may cause an immediate anaphylactoid reaction when the patient can collapse and die in seconds; this is similar to a few unfortunate people when stung by a bee for the second time. Their bodies have become sensitised by the initial sting that a further one may literally kill. If I had known that I might have been dealing with a hydatid cyst, I would have taken certain vital precautions. These would have included having potentially life saving hydrocortisone running into Chandri in the drip, to lessen this alarming reaction and more important, having adrenaline at hand – for immediate intramuscular injection. The second danger is dissemination of daughter cysts throughout the abdominal cavity; they may grow from wherever they fall and in a few months, the patient's plight could be far worse than before, with multiple cysts sprouting from anywhere. This can be minimised by injecting formal saline into the cyst following its exposure. The formaldehyde pickles the contents so that, should any escape, they are dead and cannot grow.

However in this, Chandri was lucky. In the past three months the cyst had become grossly infected to explain such a hectic fever. With the resulting pus, the contained daughter cysts had died. With antibiotics, the pus was probably sterile. She suffered no immediate reaction.

Now that the cyst had burst, the task of removing it was considerably easier. I could at least get my hands around it. It arose from the left lobe of the liver, a fairly rare site, as 75 per cent of all hydatid cysts arise from the much larger right lobe. As we have already seen, its wall was part and parcel with the diaphragm and this I had to tear to free the cyst. Even the peritoneal covering over the right kidney had to be sacrificed in order to mobilise the cyst. At last it was out and safely in a bucket. What a relief! The liver bed, however, was oozing and her lung was clearly visible through the hole in the diaphragm. Pus and the tiny hydatid cysts were swilling around in the huge space left by the cyst. I placed large warm gauze packs against the bleeding surface, while I sucked out fluid and debris from the peritoneal cavity. All this time I was meticulously careful that nothing escaped through the hole. This I quickly repaired with interrupted nylon sutures, before any foreign material could spill into her chest and later result in an empyema, a serious infection inside the chest.

I next picked out every tiny cyst I could find. Many were no bigger than my little fingernail. I removed the warm pack from the liver: there was now just a generalised ooze. I stopped this by coagulating the bleeding points with diathermy and placing an absorbable material called Sterispon against the raw area. The cyst had caused the liver to be pushed far over to the right so that the huge veins to it were stretched and angulated. I have never seen a liver so severely displaced. The cyst must have been affecting the function of the liver, by virtually strangling the blood supply. In addition, it had been pressing so hard on the bile duct that the gall bladder was large and distended.

I placed a drainage tube under the liver so that any seepage could drain away, then I closed Chandri's abdomen. I had given her two pints of blood during the operation, a ludicrously small amount, but all we had. Much blood drained through the tube during the next 18 hours, but all seemed well.

She miscarried during the night. The afterbirth, the placenta, remained inside her. She lost more blood. After long deliberation I decided (most unwisely) that she was not fit, with her damaged diaphragm, for a second general anaesthetic. I kept Chandri on large doses of Penicillin and added Streptomycin, and at first she grew stronger. The oozing from the liver stopped. I removed the tube. Chandri developed an offensive vaginal discharge. Her fever returned. I had tried ergometrine to make the womb contract. Nothing happened. Her haemoglobin dropped to 30%, a dangerously low level. I gave her another pint and changed the antibiotics. Her condition again improved and by now all her clips were out and her wound had healed well. Chandri again started to bleed through her vagina. She had not been upset in the least over the abortion. She had had no idea that she was pregnant and was perfectly content with her five children. Her haemoglobin dropped to 23%, and, more alarming, she was bleeding freely. It was not safe to wait another hour. I took her back to theatre, for an evacuation of her womb, termed a Dilatation and Curettage.

As she had been transferred from the other side of Nepal, she had no relatives to donate blood and I had only one pint to cover all emergencies. In the theatre, I started to remove the pieces of the placenta to be met by a brisk haemorrhage as if someone had turned on a tap inside her womb. The uterus was flabby from infection and would not contract, even after the immediate administration of ergometrine, through one of Chandri's veins, by Vincent Noone. My heart was pounding away. I went on scraping until I was certain that every piece of placenta had been removed, then massaged the womb until some tone returned. It started hardening at last! After a second dose of the ergometrine, the uterus contracted down quite firmly: the flood turned into a trickle and the trickle into drops and then stopped altogether. The Sister mopped my brow. The strain of those few moments had been appalling. Chandri must have lost two pints in as many minutes.

During all this, Vincent had wound the head of the operating table right down to help maintain her blood pressure by gravity. He had poured in a bottle of the blood substitute dextran, after taking a small sample of blood for cross matching. With this, I could safely test the next I could obtain, to ensure it was safe for her.

Now why did I mention dogs at the beginning of this chapter? The cause of hydatid disease and therefore of Chandri's cyst, is a tiny little worm no longer than half a centimetre, which can only be studied properly under a microscope. It has a head and four little segments, rather like a little train with carriages. This worm lives in the intestine of dogs. It is called taenia echinococcus. From the worm's last segment, eggs are being continually released which are then passed out in the faeces. The infected excreta contaminates grass where pigs, sheep and oxen may be grazing. Similarly man, by too intimate contact with his dog, or more accurately with the stools, may consume the eggs. These pass through the human intestinal wall to enter the liver, where the larval stage of the life cycle of the worm occurs, resulting in these cysts. Rarely they may pass through the liver so that the cysts are trapped and grow in the lungs. More rarely still, the larva may be pumped through a hole in the heart to reach the arteries. Then cysts may grow in any part of the body including the brain and bones.

When the sheep dies, its liver may be thrown to a dog, which becomes infected with the worm and the cycle perpetuated. Chandri, at some stage in her life, had eaten infested food and the cyst had been growing slowly over a number of years. Hopefully she would have been cured by the operation and still able to have more children!

CHAPTER 12

Water Buffalo

Thirty-one year old cowherd, Suleman, had been looking after his two buffalo in the usual manner of kneeling on the back of one of them, rather like a racing jockey.

It was February, the most pleasant time of the year, winter over, the days beginning to warm up and everything quiet and peaceful - that was, until a rogue buffalo appeared! It advanced rapidly. Suleman had been dozing peacefully on his favourite Sathi, when the two animals started fighting. In a second he was on the ground. Sathi retreated a few yards from the aggressor, which sported long, straight sharp horns, who immediately took this opportunity to gore Suleman's groin. The point passed cleanly, missing the great vessels of his thigh by a whisker, continuing under the skin all the way to his knee. It did not surprise me to hear that he had lost a pint of blood almost immediately. During this assault Suleman's other buffalo, Coghal, had been grazing happily, ignoring the tumult. The wild buffalo, deed done, retreated into the forest.

Suleman was lucky in that the attack had occurred only an hour's motor journey from us, near the Biratnager-Dharan road. Villagers, in a passing bus, collected him from the side of the road and took him to Dharan bazaar, where a landrover brought him up to the hospital. The actual wound in Suleman's skin was no bigger, or for that matter much different to the one I use for varicose vein surgery, but it was the extent of the wound under the skin that horrified me. In fact it healed perfectly and within three weeks he was out of hospital, back on Sathi, this time to keep a wary eye open – at least for the first few weeks!

Wild buffalo are very similar to domestic, only much bigger. A large bull, standing 5 foot 6 inches at the shoulder, has even been known to grow another 12 inches. He can be the most dangerous animal in the forest. Even a tiger would treat such a bull with respect. The cows are no less ferocious when with calf.

*   *   *   *   *

Balbahadur was well aware of their reputation. He was absolutely terrified when he had the misfortune to disturb two such bulls in the forest. I had heard of occasional sightings, though these were the first to cause me work. Balbahadur was sixty-nine, an old man by Nepalese standards, and had been guarding his sheep, helped by his grandchildren aged seven, eight and nine. The bulls spotted Balbahadur! They charged through the jungle straight at him. He turned and fled only to trip on the bank of a dried-up <u>nullah</u> (river bed) and crash several feet on to the rocks below. He was out of sight, his life was saved but at the cost of both a fractured forearm and femur.

His grandchildren, who fortunately had been playing some distance away, witnessed the charge and had hidden until there were no further sounds – and a lot longer too! Finally they had gone in search of grandfather and, attracted by his moans, found him in the <u>nullah</u>. They raced home and soon villagers arrived and carried Balbahadur to the side of the road. There they stopped the next bus.

These buses were a sight to be seen; more crowded than the London Underground at 'rush hour', the only difference being that there was no glass in the windows so that humanity bulged through spaces where the frames once were. Villagers clung to the sides and back as well. Many of these buses were very old and forever breaking down. Their drivers were brilliant mechanics, performing incredible feats of engineering with bits of wire, old tins and string.

Somehow they made room for Balbahadur and he reached Dharan. As he was carried from the bazaar to us, he was sprayed with red dye, this being the day of the *Holi* festivities! Finally he arrived three hours after the accident, an incredibly quick move on behalf of grandchildren, relatives and neighbours.

I fitted a temporary splint to his forearm and controlled the fractured femur by applying strapping to his leg beyond the break. To this I attached a cord, which I passed over a pulley, fixed to the end of the bed, which I had raised by putting it on blocks. I added a ten pound weight to help align the fractured bones. Two days later I inserted a Küntscher nail down the middle of his femur. Normally, though a major operation, this is a simple enough procedure, which I could do in half an hour. Not so with Balbahadur! (*The middle of any long bone is filled with bone marrow. The long tunnel inside the bone is the medullary cavity and thus no normal long bone is ever truly solid. Most men have a large medullary cavity to their femur, the largest and longest bone in the body. We choose the size of the Küntscher nail to be inserted, by first measuring the length of the sound femur and then strapping the nail to that thigh for an x-ray. By comparing the width of the medullary cavity with the breadth of the selected nail, on the film, we can accurately find a nail of the correct size*). Balbahadur's cavity looked very small indeed, only large enough to take an 8 mm nail. However, as I searched for this in the broken bones, it simply didn't appear to exist. I had to ream it out to take even the finest nail. I have never tackled a more difficult nailing and the operation took me three times as long as usual. I next manipulated the fractured forearm, putting his arm in an above elbow plaster.   He was none the worse for my efforts and went home happily, on crutches, a month later, once his radius and ulna had united.

*   *   *   *   *

What a lucky little girl was Chauri! The twelve-year old was feeding her buffalo when she received the injury that came within an ace of killing her. Her family owned eight of these animals and it was Chauri's job to look after them.   That evening, Chauri had been delayed and one buffalo was extremely angry at his late supper. He vented his wrath by tossing his head. A horn pierced her side, ripping open her stomach so severely that the contents spilt.

Her father applied yellow <u>sindur</u> (a dye) to the protruding mass. (<u>Sindur</u> is thought to stop bleeding by the villagers.) He covered the area with kapok, a fine cotton-like white fluffy material surrounding seeds of a tree, (normally used to stuff pillows).

They were fortunate to have a Gurkha pensioner in the village who had once worked in a medical centre in the Army. He warned that Chauri's condition was so serious that they must get her to hospital as quickly as possible. He applied flavine, instead of the kapok, and gave Chauri an injection before urging them on their way. Chauri was carried by four relatives in a <u>doli,</u> (hammock) thirty-six miles in twenty-four hours. They ran most of the way. (In the mountains that was a wonderful feat of endurance.)

As I examined Chauri, the first thing I established was that she did not have peritonitis. Her abdomen was soft to my touch, which caused her little pain. Whatever was sticking out was also acting as an effective plug, no germs had entered in.

80

When I took down the dressing I found a haemorrhagic mass which was so discoloured that I couldn't guess what it might be. I set up a transfusion and, under general anaesthetic, opened up the wound. My first surprise was that the buffalo horn had ended up between the 9th and 10th ribs. It had missed her heart and lung by less than one inch; of course, if it hadn't, I simply would never have heard of Chauri!

Had the horn damaged the diaphragm? This is the muscle we use for breathing. It lies between the abdomen and the chest; if this had been perforated, it might have resulted in an empyema, a near fatal complication in a primitive country. I asked my anaesthetist to close the gas escape valve to allow the bag to fill. I then asked him to squeeze it. If there were a hole in the lung, air would bubble out. There was no hole. Again Chauri had been lucky.

The next organ I examined was the spleen. This is a purplish organ, the size of a hand, which is situated under the ribs on the left-hand side of the abdomen. As far as I knew, at the time, the spleen has little function in an adult, yet its damage has been the cause of countless deaths, usually as a complication of a road traffic accident. Haemorrhage from the spleen can be so severe that the only treatment is immediate operation to remove the organ. (*Many years later I was to learn that the spleen has, in fact, vital functions and we now do our best to preserve even a ruptured spleen, if possible*). The organ is so deeply placed that injury to it may not be detected early enough, with fatal consequences. I enlarged Chauri's wound to explore her inside. Here again she had been lucky for the horn had missed the spleen as well.

And what was the protruding organ? It was the faithful old "policeman of the abdomen" (an apron of fat, called the omentum.) Once again this organ had saved another life, by effectively sealing the hole made by the horn. All I had to do was to remove the contaminated portion and close the wounds. I was very relieved.

Next day I was not so happy. Chauri was running a temperature and her pulse was rapid. I assumed that the wound must have been infected after all. I simply continued the antibiotic therapy and fed her through an intravenous infusion to rest the abdominal contents. There were still no signs of peritonitis and already the intestines had recovered from the double assault of buffalo and knife. By the third day Chauri was eating happily, but her temperature and pulse remained obstinately high. I examined the wound; there was no infection. I ordered a chest x-ray and there, to my dismay, were collapsed lobes of her lung. Had I missed a hole in the diaphragm after all? "Oh dear!" I sighed. "But Sir," said the radiographer, "there are your dressings!" The collapse was opposite to her gored chest. Now each piece of gauze used at operation has a radio-opaque tag so that, should a swab inadvertently be left behind, the marker can be picked up by x-ray. A retained swab can cause serious complications such as sepsis and obstructed bowel, even leading to death. What we saw on the x-ray had no mark and had simply been used to cover the wound!

I went back to Chauri to enquire, once more, exactly what she had been doing at the time of the accident. She then remembered how she had been chewing nuts as she had approached the irate buffalo. The shock of the horn had caused her to gasp and inhale the nuts, which now lodged in her right main bronchus. This had partially blocked, so that the lower half of her lung had later collapsed. No wonder she had a temperature! She was so fit otherwise that her respiration rate had not increased, in spite of the obstruction.

Having diagnosed the cause, the cure was clear. I took her pillows away and raised the bottom of her bed by placing it on blocks. I forced her to cough. "<u>Kok</u>," I cried, thumping her chest with the edge of my hands. "<u>Kok</u>, <u>Kok</u>, <u>Kok</u>." I was determined to make her chest expand. She put up with my administrations without a murmur, and whenever I was in the ward I repeated the exercise. In addition, I made her lean over the side of her bed in an attempt to dislodge the nuts by gravity. Two days later she coughed violently; one of her lobes had re-expanded. She proudly presented me with a piece of nut when I was next on the ward. The following day the middle lobe of her lung had also recovered as she produced a second. Her lung had now fully expanded. Her pulse rate and her temperature had returned to normal. The physiotherapy was over! Just eight days after her admission, we were able to send her home.

RELAXATION

A young girl chased by <u>bhalu</u> (bear).

CHAPTER 13

Breakfast with Everest

We set off for the Sanguri Chalet, in the foothills of the Himalayas, in the middle of the monsoon, but had to turn back after being too frightened to cross a river. A tree was conveniently uprooted halfway across the water, but although we were able to climb along this, the swirling current now reached chest height. We decided to abandon the trip. It was frightening to see the level visibly rising with the rain and to realise how the Nepalese must risk their lives carrying the sick across such rivers to reach the hospital.

As we retraced our steps, we passed columns of men and women, returning from market, loaded with matches, salt, kerosene, umbrellas, cloth and all kinds of kitchen utensils. It started to rain again so Anna and I put up our umbrellas, along with many of the Nepalese we passed. It seemed incongruous to see a man, dressed in rags, holding up a smart black umbrella! Incidentally, many of their loads were protected from the rain by sheets of polythene.

Caravans of porters and travellers begin to move as dawn breaks, though the majority cook the first of their two meals a day and set off when properly light, as the paths can be treacherous. The villagers do not appear to mind where they sleep, so I have had to step over sleeping forms on the occasions I have travelled at night. Nor do the Nepalese appear to mind where they relieve themselves, and it can be very unpleasant to leave the main track to enter a shady nook! The monsoon is also the time for common leech when up to 30 of these blood sucking worms may collect at the end of a frond waiting for the next passing victim. In addition there are tree leeches, which drop on you. Beware too if you have to squat down with a bare bottom!

Each porter carries a strong 'T' shaped stick, which he uses as a walking stick and to support his load when he rests, which he does frequently. He simply props the bottom of his basket on the horizontal portion and leans back; nearly all the weight is taken, while he has a post to lean back on. Porters don't mind where they stop; inevitably bang in the middle of the path. These tracks are often very narrow that although Anna and I could easily dodge in and out of a line of resting porters, (who, rather disconcertingly, always stared open-mouthed at us), our own loaded porters could not.

These Nepali, who hike across the Himalyan mountains carrying more than their own body weight, are without doubt the world's greatest porters. Part of their immense skill is achieved by "taking their time".

Seeing a European is good enough excuse for a chat. "Where are you going? Where have you come from?" they always begin. Apart from that, I could understand little of what they said. This disgusted the Nepalese who have no time for anyone who does not speak their language.

One weekend, in November 1966, we set off again to try to see Mount Everest, with Narbahadur carrying James, then ten months, in a wicker basket, and a porter, loaded with our sleeping bags, blankets and hurricane lamps.

The river was now just a stream but the three hour climb to the 5,000 feet châlet was exhausting, though the baby laughed all the way. We finally passed through a little village where green and red parrots called to us and where we bought and filled our pockets with tangerines, the size of oranges. Their juice was so refreshing it gave us renewed energy.

The châlet, established by the Nuffield Trust, was perfectly situated, having two panoramic views of the Himalayas. There were three bedrooms, a kitchen and a living room with an enormous fireplace. It was bitterly cold compared with the 90°F (32°C) in Dharan and we were in cloud much of the time. Wood is plentiful on the surrounding mountainside and it was splendid to have our first fire of the year. (Incidentally, this is leopard country.)

At six o'clock we got up, freezing, to admire the sun rise over the Himalayas. The sky is usually crystal clear in the early morning and the mountains looked cold and austere. As dawn broke, the Kanchejunga (28,209 feet) range to the East was picked up by the pink of the sun and the whole scene started to take life. As the sun rose higher, this turned to blue while the Western panorama lit up. First Makalu, (27,824), then Pethangtse, (22,060), next Lhotse, (27,890), came to life, until finally the sun shone only on Everest (*Sagarmatha*) 29,035, eighty-five miles away yet the only peak in the whole panorama to be "flood lit"; no theatrical electrician could have made the effect more dramatic. After a few minutes, as the sun rose higher, the mountains returned to their bleak, forbidding selves. We were now grateful for our thick sweaters and bowls of steaming porridge, as we tried to warm up after this our first glimpse of Everest, now just a peak guarded by Chamlong, (24,012), to one side with Lhotse on the other. Once the show was over, we left the cold of the châlet for the warmth of Dharan. There, waiting for me, after my "night off," was a lady needing a Caesarian Section and a man requiring fixing of a fractured femur. I could never be away for more than a few hours – this was very frustrating. This had been my first "night off" in seven months in the country.

It is on Kanchejunga that the 5 to 6 inch "snowball" plants are found, a thick altitude thistle, covered with what looks like cotton wool, that keeps the temperature in the plant 15 degreees warmer than outside. Because of this, bees have been seen to fly in and out of a hole in this cover at an altitude of 17,000 feet.

Lower, are giant stinging nettles – 10 foot tall – which have been described as a "vegetable rottweiler" because of the ferocity of their sting. They are used to make rope, while the tender leaves are eaten. Giant rhubarb plants have 4 foot fronds. Cannabis grows on the slopes. Between 10 – 12,000 feet are juniper trees, sacred to the Buddhist, who believe spirits live in them. These trees reach a great age.

A lily (Arisaema) can look exactly like a rearing cobra, while the pealing bark of the silver birch has been called "King's paper" and used as parchment. Alpine plants grow very well in yak pasteurs at 12 – 15,000 feet. Some look like oxlip. Moss and fern grow on the trunks and branches of trees in the high humidity and orchids are collected to decorate many a village home.

River crossing.

CHAPTER 14

A Day in the Market

Goitre

Friday and Saturday are market days in Dharan bazaar, and during the winter months the market is a blaze of colour.

Anna and I occasionally used to stroll through the market. We started at the silversmiths, who squat down with their bags of East India Company silver, charging ten rupees (50p) for an 1834 William IV rupee, eight for an early Victorian rupee and five and a half for one of 1900. Many of the coins are devoid of commercial value because a clip that has been soldered on so that they can be worn. Coins have been strung together to form a large necklace. The size of the coins: rupee, half rupee, or quarter rupee, worn by the women, seems to depend on their age, so that the little girls look enchanting sporting their long chain of quarter pieces.

The silversmiths also sell large Chinese dollars collected from a bygone era, when trade with Tibet was flourishing. Large blocks of solid silver were available, as were old Tibetan silver ornaments, brought down by refugees and sold when food had become the priority of life. Huge silver bracelets were on offer though few were solid silver. There were similar anklets and necklaces.

Gold is very popular, there being such a strong distrust of paper currency that the majority of the villagers' wealth was held in jewellery - ear-rings, necklaces and nose rings which the wives sported. The Nepalese were also loath to leave valuables in their homes, so these were worn whenever practical. Solid gold was also for sale, measured in tolas or half tolas. A tola was worth four hundred Nepalese rupees and the best insurance for a time when ready cash was needed.

From the silversmiths we visited the stainless-steel shop. The goods were actually manufactured in Biratnager. We bought six little dishes, at four rupees each, to hold grapefruit. Sadly this did not appear to grow in Nepal, so ours came up with the weekly order from Calcutta. They were useful in the evening to trap "creepy crawlies" which used to terrify Anna. It was the bearer's job to dispatch them at dawn.

One morning, I had to perform a "matador's twist" to avoid the horns of a cow which was running amok through the market, scattering tangerines and vegetables in all directions. That same day I saw a lady whose right eye had been destroyed by an advanced cancer, an epithelioma, that it had spread across the bridge of her nose to within half an inch of the other eye. Soon she would be blind in both. It had progressed too far for surgery and was now inoperable. Without radiotherapy, I could do nothing. There was, of course, no such service in the whole of Nepal. On another occasion I noticed a man who had lost a hand. I asked what had happened. He was now sixty-two and, when a young man of twenty, had been cutting grass in the jungle when bitten by a king cobra. He immediately struck off his hand, with his kukri, thus undoubtedly saving his life.

Next we saw a lady with the end results of burns to her face and hands. Her fingers were already snarled up. As the facial burns had healed, scar tissue had pulled down her lower eyelids – a condition called ectropion – so that she was unable to close her eyes. The lower half of both were thus permanently exposed to the air. In addition, she couldn't sleep with her eyes properly closed, so that they were already red. Dryness and infection would lead inevitably to blindness. Surgery for such a condition often results in further scarring.

However, I did do some good that morning. A brother and sister came to me; the man with an old kukri wound to his wrist which had severed the main nerve to his hand, the median nerve, and the woman had a double harelip. I invited the two to attend my clinic at the B.M.H., because I could help them both.

The market is full of different tribes and nationalities including Tibetans, usually in native dress, and of course Indians. On one occasion I visited the market with Brigadier Richard Hunt, then Consultant Surgeon to the Far East. He told me how, in that same market, on a previous visit, he had been pestered by Tibetans, who were fascinated by the long white hairs on his forearms and chest. They kept plucking them, oblivious to his feeling. Tibetans and Nepalese rarely have hair on their arms, chest, faces, or for that matter anywhere, apart from their heads! The Brigadier terrified them by setting off the alarm to his wrist-watch.

Most of the fruit is carried down to the market in baskets on the backs of the villagers, beautifully packed with large leaves separating the different layers. The best tangerines cost 1p each while the larger, older ones ½p. The Indians try to buy the fruit in bulk to resell at a higher price in the same market. For this reason we were most particular from whom we made our purchases. Business men took the tangerines and oranges down to India to make fruit juice.

I was very touched to be presented with two huge lemons by a villager. I had operated on his father. Lettuces, cabbages, garlic, tomatoes, new potatoes, onions, carrots, red and green chillies were all plentiful.

Honey looked most appetising. Dollops of honeycomb were placed on large leaves. Huge loads of cinnamon leaves were carried into the market - so enormous that I couldn't even see the bearer's head!

At the butchers,we bought 4 lbs of wild boar leg for eight rupees; wrapped in large green sal leaves. I bought an earthenware pot for one rupee into which I placed the meat. The bowl, with the leaves, protected the joint from flies and dirt, as well as keeping it remarkably cool. I was duly impressed by his skill cutting chops with his kukri, though found them rather too fatty for my liking. The local pigs' hair is black and thick; it is dried in the sun to be made in to shoe brushes.

The results following surgery.

The next man I passed had a large haemangioma, a blood vessel tumour, situated in the region where children develop mumps. This affliction appears to be remarkably common in Nepal. As I examined him he complained of <u>duca</u>, pain, but I have learned, from bitter experience, how difficult these are to remove. As the tumours are literally a mass of blood vessels, the operation is extremely hazardous.

The lady from whom I bought peas had a huge enlargement of one side of her thyroid gland. Premkedah, my senior theatre orderly, told me how he had already tried to get her to see me but she had been far too frightened. She was only one of the many sufferers of goitre whom I saw most days, but a great character. Her goitre had reached the size of a melon. Udai Sing had himself repeatedly advised her to come, as he bought his peas week after week. Then I came with mine, but still she would not come! A week later, she confessed to Udai that her great fear was that, if she had an operation, she would die, but he smiled and warned her that if she did not come she would suffocate.

"Then I will die?" she had asked. "Yes," Udai had replied bluntly, "you will die."

We had still not finished the negotiations. Three times she sent her husband, who himself sported a large goitre, to discuss her problems before finally consenting herself. Meanwhile I removed her husband's! His wife's lump had indeed become so serious that her voice was already hoarse, as the tumour pressed on the nerves in her neck and compressed her trachea. I gave her iodine, in an attempt to shrink it, with iron and vitamins to make her as fit as possible.

She was finally admitted and … eleven days later was back in the market, selling peas! She had only had to be in hospital six days. Her neck was flat, her swelling, and perhaps a little of her appeal, had gone.

"Well," said Udai, next market day, "see, you are still alive." She smiled. I'm pretty sure he got free peas until the end of the season.

We next entered a tailor's shop for a couple of shoulder bags called jolas and a kapok-filled eiderdown which I planned to make into a sleeping-bag for James, should we go up to the châlet again. In fact it ended up as a cover to one of the easy wicker garden chairs, I used to recline on, for satellite watching.

There was a sewing-machine in every tailor's shop which was worked by foot. On the whole the tailors were good though few totally honest. Though their prices were low, they tended to skimp on material, keeping the excess.

The market had its lighter side, with even the occasional performing bear. There were caged birds that could "tell" your fortune. About a dozen tiny birds live in separate cells, contained in a larger wooden cage about a foot high and eighteen inches wide. For a few pice, I was asked my name and a little bird hopped down from his little home, as the fortune-teller opened the door. The bird picked up an envelope from a large number in front; this he discarded; he selected a second and from it removed a card which was presented to me. It read: "you are very happy at present and things are going very well, but something will change in the next few months." Anna was two months pregnant at the time, so I assumed that this message meant the new arrival – not, I fervently hoped, sleepless nights! A few days later Anna had a threatened miscarriage; she had to stay in bed a fortnight. This was to happen twice more during the pregnancy. These were worrying times! All was well eventually and Rachel was born, none the worse for earlier scares.

Pet birds were also for sale, including green parakeets (like Percy, our own who lived on the verandah), large beautiful green parrots, and occasionally the yellow-beaked black hill mynah. These were fantastic mimics.

Book sellers were numerous and their shelves were full of stories about the gods including the hero Rama. Towards the end of my two years I saw 'The Thoughts of Mao' prominently displayed on most stalls.

Most women wear their hair in plaits. Black and red materials were sold in this form, in order to make their hair appear longer, a sign of beauty.

Part of the market stank from decomposing tiny fish. These had been caught in their thousands by the villagers dragging nets through streams and lakes. I never tried them myself – they looked disgusting. They are however an important source of iodine and can reduce goitre.

For a long time I couldn't understand why all the taps in the market were left running. I put this down to the extraordinary casualness of the Nepalese over this precious commodity. I subsequently learned that Bahuns and Chettris could not possibly handle taps that had been touched by a lower caste! Thus the water pours away, as in the Gurkha lines in the cantonment.

Little flutes, made from bamboo canes, were on sale for the young, while long sticks of sugar-cane were as eagerly sought as sweets back home.

Anna and I finished our visit by watching an old man smoking opium. Though illegal, this was being sold openly in the market.

As the traders had made this long trek from the hills to earn a few rupees, they marked the occasion for a well-earned rest ending with a dance. At this much <u>rakshi</u> is consumed --- so Saturday night at the hospital was much the same as the Accident and Emergency Unit back home!

CHAPTER 15

Christmas

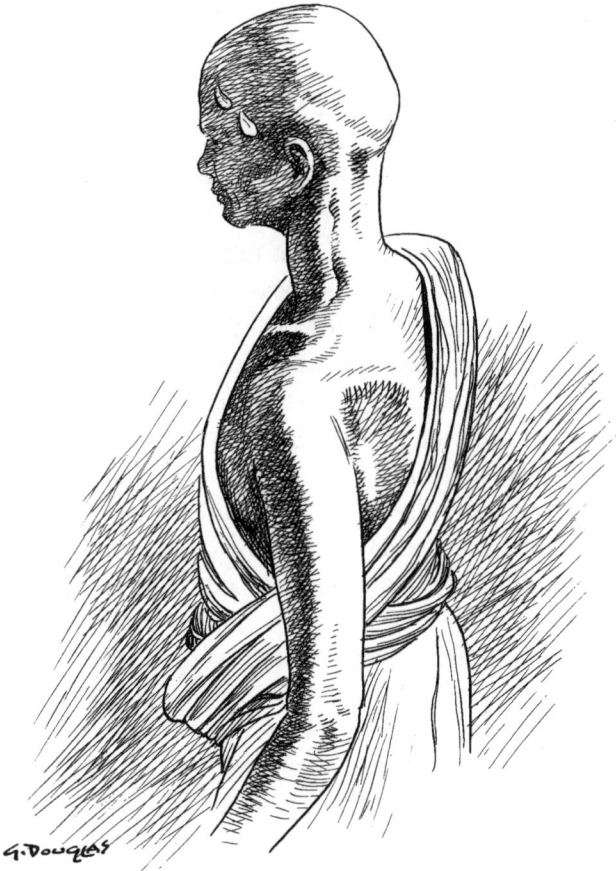

A widow who has consulted the witch doctor.
(Note leaves stuck on temple).

Christmas was a happy, colourful occasion, but also important, as it was the only time in the year that we could act as missionaries, (apart from goodwill and example throughout the rest of the year). Preaching the gospel was banned by the King.

The ward Sisters, as at home, took on responsibility for the decorations. In the Families ward, Captain June Pickering placed a baby, born six days earlier by Caesarean Section, in a crib. The infant, wrapped in a shawl and lying on straw, was a most touching sight. Without the presence of the hospital, that baby would never have been born alive. Almost a week earlier, we had had to rush his mother straight to the theatre, within five minutes of arrival. The baby's arm, (not the head as it should have been), was protruding. There was a huge risk that, at any moment, the umbilical cord would descend with it. If this had happened, and the cord, the lifeline, compressed, the baby would have died within a few minutes. Also, it would have been impossible for the mother to have delivered even a dead baby in such a position. Both would have perished.

Babies coming out in twisted positions are more common in grand multigravida – that is mothers having their sixth or subsequent delivery. By then, the abdominal muscles have been so stretched by carrying this number, that nature cannot always guide the baby perfectly down the birth canal. This mother looked incredibly young, yet she had had her six already!

She had first discovered the baby's arm, eight long hours earlier, at 4 o'clock in the morning. By the time we saw her, the arm was blue and swollen from compression. A large area of skin had been rubbed off the bend of his elbow due to chafing against the mother's thigh. We knew that the baby was alive, as the little hand gripped June's finger. This phenomenon is known as the "grasp reflex" and all babies, up to a few months, will automatically grasp anything put into their hands. It is not every day that we can demonstrate this in an unborn baby! The operation had gone smoothly and by Christmas Day both mother and baby were well on the way to recovery, and the swollen arm had largely recovered.

The theme for the Male ward was "Streets". Jean Bruce-Gardyne, the nursing Sister and gifted artist, had chosen the McIntosh Quality Street, with "Welcome to Quality Street" displayed above the door. She had drawn the characters on the tin in life size, painted them and stuck them on the walls. Quality Street led into Limbu (a Nepalese tribe) Lane, and the side-rooms, off the main corridor, were variously labelled. On the sluice door was "Bruce-Gardyne and Pickering, Delivery Agents, twenty-four hour service, you call, we come." (These two nursing Sisters ran our midwifery department.) Another was labelled "M. Banahan, Florist, Seasonal Blooms, Bed Pansies, Asthmas, Double Pneumonias, Hysterias, Scabies." (Mike, the senior medical officer, was in charge of both administration and medical wards.) "D. Gent, Carpenter: Stools a "Speciality" described our Pathology technician; the next was labelled: "P. Pitt and Son, Family Butcher: Special cuts to order". A sign on another described the Roman Catholic priest: "Mr. Shock, Cobbler: Heels taken in and Souls repaired."

The Surgical ward was named Bahun Buildings, S.E.1. while Rai Road led to the Medical ward at Chettri Close, S.W.1. Jean's office was labelled "Dharan Police Station" where, on the "wanted list", was a description of Father Christmas. The most frequented room was "Mother Brown's Cake Shop", for this was where refreshments were served. Madge was our very popular Matron.

The ward was decorated with scenes of reindeer and sleighs and the nursing orderlies had had a fine time putting up

101

streamers and blowing up balloons. The two Tuberculosis wards, also under Jean's auspices, looked most attractive. The Himalayas had been reproduced with cotton wool against a dark blue background – a sheet draped over screens.

Vincent, the anaesthetist ("V. Noone, mattress-maker, guarantees you perfect sleep") was dressed as Father Christmas, placed on a trolley and pulled round the wards by enthusiastic helpers. It was very touching to see the little children's faces as Father Christmas politely greeted all and sundry with <u>namaste</u>, before presenting each with a stocking loaded with presents. Everyone in the hospital received one, many several.

The tour started on the Families ward where the mother, who had the Caesarean Section, was first to receive a present. He next turned to a frail old lady, who was sitting out in an armchair for the first time since she carried to hospital. She wasn't really old, being only sixty, but was a widow and it is Hindu custom that her head had to be shorn. Although this made her look older, it was the awful mental and physical anguish she had been through in the past few days, that had aged her most. She and a friend had climbed a tree to cut down leaves. By the cruellest fate, a Himalayan black bear was in the same tree. Her companion's face had been ripped to ribbons by the long claws of the irate bear, who next plunged its teeth into her side. A few moments later she was dead. In stark terror, our patient had fallen out of the tree, crashing heavily on her hip. Her head had simultaneously struck the ground and mercifully she blacked out. She was unmolested. The bear left her for dead. She had arrived in great pain and a week before Christmas, I had operated upon her hip. Much the best present she had that day, was my allowing her out of bed.

The Hindus have cruel customs for widows, who may only wear white apparel. No jewellery is permitted. Even what they eat is restricted. Meat, eggs, onions and even <u>dahl</u> are taboo.

Many have found a way round this. When young, the girl is married to a tree! Should her husband die, she need not suffer these deprivations, as still technically married – if only to the tree.

Father Christmas approached another old lady, who had had the largest abdomen I have ever seen, yet now, on Christmas Day, it was quite flat. The swelling had so pushed up her diaphragm, that every breath had been laboured. There just hadn't been enough room inside to take the huge mass, her womb had actually been pushed out. It had lain grotesquely between her legs, a condition termed "complete procidentia". Even her umbilicus had popped out like an orange. The veins that collect the blood from the legs and abdomen were obstructed, and as a result, her legs were swollen like tree trunks. She had been a pitiable sight; life had been a total burden. I suspected that she must have had an ovarian cyst, and prayed it might be benign.

I had previously removed three huge ovarian cysts weighing twenty-one, twenty and eighteen pounds, and I was sure that this one would break all these records. The world record is one-hundred-and-thirty-one pounds. That weighed more than what was left of the patient! But we were not to break any records. As I opened her, gallons of fluid flooded out. The actual cyst weighed a mere ten pounds – the rest was just water! That morning the report had arrived from Singapore, where we sent all our specimens for analysis, it was benign. The swelling had gone, she could breathe normally, she could live again. She was delighted. She had slim ankles. She could even walk home with the help of a ring pessary.

Father Christmas next visited a lady suffering from tuberculous peritonitis. I had not known what was wrong with her but my diagnostic laparotomy had immediately determined the cause. Nowadays, this is a extremely rare in England, but in Nepal, it was all too common. In six weeks she would feel a new woman with the help of streptomycin, para-aminosalicylic acid and isoniazid, which cured all but the most resistant case. The tablets must be taken for at least a year, but would they be?

We were never without a "burns" victim, and true enough that Christmas was Deomaya, a little girl who had thus lost her leg. She was far too young to appreciate her stocking but her mother was thrilled with her five rupee string of pearls! Madge Brown had been most diplomatic and every mother on the ward was given these; they were a wonderful success.

As most were still breast-feeding, we allowed them to stay in the ward. Their presence is a huge help to the nurses for there is rarely an occasion when the staff have to feed a child. The mother does everything.

They become very adaptable to ward routine at bedtime. By far the most popular place is curled up with the baby in its cot! One, when told that she must no longer do this, simply slept on the floor under the cot, having first taken the baby out to join her! How the babies were never suffocated amazed me, for even the new-born share their mothers' bed; we never had a cot death; mothers were not at all keen on the little maternity cots provided, they were too small to share! Two armchairs pushed together make an alternative bed, otherwise three hard chairs together, a bench or a table were perfectly acceptable to women who normally sleep on mud floors anyway.

There were other luxuries wherever they slept, for in summer, were fans, and in winter, blankets and central heating. But most important, was food. The cooks prepared vast quantities, (anything left over being fed to the pigs, which must have been the fattest and best nourished in Nepal.) I was amazed at how much and how quickly the mothers consumed their food. Huge mounds of rice would disappear in seconds, all by hand, the right hand, the left being used for the other purpose. The basic hospital diet was rice, served at every meal. To this was added <u>dahl</u>, like sieved lentils, and vegetables. (In winter, cauliflower, potatoes, beans, peas and carrots all grow abundantly.) The protein is chicken, goat or pork.

In the tropics, - chicken, duck or goose – are sold alive. In the heat, not only will meat go off very quickly, once the bird is killed, but there is a lot of disease amongst the fowl so you cannot be certain how the bird had died unless you see it killed.

But to return to Father Christmas's round. A five-year-old boy had been helping his mother cook their evening meal. He had been blowing glowing embers of the mud stove when suddenly it back fired and he was severely burned on his chin and neck. He was momentarily terrified by Father Christmas's beard but, after receiving his stocking, knew he was on to a good thing and followed Vincent round the rest of the hospital.

We were also never without a patient with a fractured femur, and that Christmas-tide, a ten-year-old girl had got up in the middle of the night to pay a call to nature. She had fallen the ten feet off the first storey of her house, as she missed her footing in the dark. I had treated her broken thighbone by inserting a Steimann pin, a strong, thin, pointed steel rod through the bone below the knee. To this I attached a stirrup and to that a cord which I hung over a pulley at the end of her bed. To the cord I tied seven pounds in weight. We next put blocks under the end of the bed to lift it up. This form of traction held the bones in perfect alignment, while nature did the rest: only five to six weeks at such a tender age. A few days later, I heard squeals of laughter coming from her bed. Four nurses were clustered round her head, hunting for fleas! There is no shame to have fleas in Nepal. The girls wear their hair very long and rarely wash it. They live in such unhygienic conditions that their heads are often alive with the insects. It is a very happy pastime, sitting out in the sun, hunting fleas; it whiles away the hours and is very satisfying to the sufferer!

Houses on stilts, the cattle, goats and chicken being underneath.

The next to be visited was again too young to appreciate the occasion. Every day her mother was benefiting from the stay. The little girl, nineteen days old on Christmas Day, had suffered from septicaemia. Bacteria had settled in her shoulder blade and caused acute osteomyelitis. From there infection had spread into her shoulder joint resulting in acute pyogenic arthritis (abscess in the joint). Pus had entered her blood. She was covered in boils. Her mother's condition was likewise very weak. Not only had she been bleeding virtually non-stop since delivery, but she had suffered severe dysentery, complicating her anaemia. Finally, she was riddled with worms. Both were now well on the way to recovery. Pearls were just the treat to make her totally content.

It was at this early stage that I was called away to reception to see yet another ill baby –I couldn't witness the happy faces of all the patients, but I had seen enough; the story of Father Christmas would be recounted in dozens of villages for weeks to come.

That evening, having put out all the lights, we led a procession of Sisters, Nurses and Nursing Orderlies round the wards and corridors of the hospital, singing Christmas carols, by hurricane lamp. The singing was enjoyed by one and all. Finally, we congregated in the Sisters' mess for hot mince pies and coffee.

Later that evening, a group of school children came to our home. We invited them in to sing carols, playing music on home made instruments including a harmonium. They sang beautifully while their bright little brown eyes were agog at the luxuries around– especially the lit up Christmas tree covered with decorations and presents.

The inevitable happened. They woke James, then eleven months old. Having got over his astonishment at the room full of children, he was immediately at ease. He soon joined in lustily with his version of how it should be sung. He was particularly intrigued by a goat-skin drum one young lady was beating, and the tinkling bracelets the girls were wearing.

As he grew older he used to have long chats, in Nepalese, with Brigadier Tony Taggart, whenever they met. We shudder to think what secrets he might have disclosed!

CHAPTER 16

Epilepsy

It was over this same Christmas period that we first met an extraordinary young man. He was limping through the cantonment with a dirty bandage on his heel, after apparently sitting outside my house most of the afternoon – much to the consternation of Jill who swore she could smell rotting flesh! When I asked what was the matter, he was very slow in replying. He had a peculiar, haunting stare. As I was getting nowhere, I told him to come to my Outpatients' in two days' time. We were just setting out for the nine-lesson carol service when Anna screamed. She had seen a face pressed against the French window. It was that man again. He told me he wanted to sleep in my house! I took him over to reception, where, the orderly told me, he had been twice already that night, he had asked the guards to take him away, but simply returned. I told the orderly to take down the dressings and if his sores were really serious, to admit him. If it were a hoax, he was to drive him away a third and final time. Jill had been right about the smell! It came from a very serious deep burn over his heel and ankle, which had happened three months earlier. He told us he had walked from Assam on this rotten leg, a distance of at least a hundred miles and had not eaten for five days. When he had arrived at Dharan bazaar, he had been told of the B.M.H. and determined to be admitted. I assumed his odd behaviour was due to a combination of: starvation, fatigue, but, on further evidence, due to his damaged brain from uncontrolled epileptic convulsions for many years.

We dressed his leg every day applying the yellow antiseptic flavine. All appeared to be going well until one day I heard him ranting and raving. The orderlies had just pulled him off fifteen-year-old Tikaram, recovering from a double fractured leg – which he had suffered a month earlier.

I soon put an end to the ravings by such a heavy dose of sedation (ten cubic centimetres of paraldehyde into his buttock) that he slept the rest of that day. I further sedated him with large doses of phenobarbitone so that, not only would he be too sleepy for further assaults, but future epileptic fits might be minimised. There was no further physical violence. His burns soon became much cleaner. After a few days, I was able to take skin from behind his thigh; to me the easiest place to obtain a large graft, it provides a flat surface for the knife to slide over. I cut this sheet of skin into pieces, the same size as the conventional postage-stamp, and placed them on the raw area, hoping that, in the presence of infection, some at least might take. He was lucky. His leg began to heal quickly. Then one day his mother arrived. She was extremely agitated. She had been looking everywhere for him. Apparently he had been treated in the little Government hospital in Dharan all the time and had absconded. She was most relieved to find him.

The lad continued to act strangely. He kept rubbing his heel up and down the bed, knocking off the dressings as if he didn't want it to heal! He also started having further fits, even while on phenobarbitone. I added epanutin, a second anticonvulsant drug; we put his leg in a below-knee walking-plaster so that he could neither scratch nor rub it. We were then able to discharge him, under the care of his mother, much to the relief of staff and patients. A month later he returned. I removed the plaster. His leg had healed at last, after five long months. Would he leave it alone now it was healed? I never saw him again. I just don't know.

CHAPTER 17

Madness

Madness is a serious problem in Nepal as there are few, if any, institutions for its management; that is, apart from prison. A rather sweet-faced young lady of twenty calmly walked through my open French windows one afternoon while I was showing cine-films. I sat her down to watch a film of James' christening and an elephant ride that Anna and I had been on. I gave her a snack and guided her out through the kitchen door once the show was over. She came back through the front door two minutes later! I asked Narbahadur to lead her away, only for her to reappear at the same French windows minutes later. I took her to a chair on the outside verandah and suggested she sat down. This she did, for about half an hour, until she got bored, and came inside again. After she finally left, I quickly locked all the doors and windows!

She had never been aggressive but Jill was not best pleased to discover that she had taken her bikini bottom!. The following night, which happened to be full moon, she had been seen by the water tower stripped to the waist. Later she appeared, still topless, at a dinner-party at one of the homes. This led to cryptic remarks about "floor-shows"!

Things got more serious when she smashed four panes to break into the British Officers' Mess and made her bed on the billiard-table.

"But she didn't sign the visitors' book!" cried the anguished mess secretary, Major Bond.

The police were called to take her away. One appeared at my Sick Parade next day with a huge haematoma (bruise) in his groin where she had kneed him viciously.

She seemed to have an affinity for the billiard-table, as she broke in again the next night by breaking further panes, to make her bed on the table a second time.

We heard no more until a month later. It was full moon. Yet again she broke into the Officers' Mess; this time she laid out all the mess silver on the dining-room floor. She proceeded to take a strip wash in the gentlemen's cloak room and finally settled down in the ladies' room for the night. In truth her antics would have been tolerated, if only she had not broken windows. They took the young lady to Biratnager gaol, but this, by then, had fallen to pieces! She had to be released, so she returned to stay with her brother, who worked in the cantonment and all was peaceful – until the next full moon, when again she broke in. This was lunacy!

We paid her brother to take her back to his village. This he did and her story, as far as we were concerned at the British Officers' Mess, was over. I was rather sad. She had certainly woken up the old camp!

TO THE HILLS

Bhag (leopard) stealing a pig.

CHAPTER 18

Darjeeling

This had been Anna's second visit to Darjeeling. The first had been with Major Mike Banahan and Claire Noone, my anaesthetist's wife. They had gone the whole way by landrover. While Anna was in Darjeeling, she had a strong sense of déja vu, quite different to anything she had ever experienced.

Anna had been adopted and years later our youngest, Daniel, born in England in 1969, and now a barrister in Family Law in chambers in Cambridge, traced her birth mother: Amy Fell, who had gone to live near Darjeeling, with a tea planter, following Anna's adoption. She had died six months before Daniel completed his mission – which Anna felt must have been a relief to Betty, her adopted mother and perhaps herself.

Anna and I decided to take my first vacation after we had been in the country a year. We had planned our holiday months in advance but this had been shattered by Anna's abortion and threatened miscarriages while carrying Rachel. At last we could visit Darjeeling. To go the whole way by landrover would be too risky to her health, so we planned instead to make the journey partly by landrover, mostly by train and finally by taxi. The train arrived at Katihar, at the wretched hour of half-past-six in the morning, so we went to bed at 8 o'clock in preparation for a 2am departure. The station was a four-hour landrover drive. Anna was up at 1 a.m to prepare our picnic breakfast and lunch.

Transport arrived fifteen minutes early and we all bundled in, with Doma holding James, our cases in a trailer behind. We sped down the road, looking out for wild life but all we saw was a rabbit!

Eventually we reached Biratnager, on the Nepalese side of the border. The checkpoint is simply a pole across the road. With great difficulty, after waking several others, we managed to find a very sleepy, dirty-looking old man. This was the officer in charge. He shambled out of his bed to be told by our driver that we had nothing to declare. He let us through with no more ado. Anna said a disparaging "good morning", to be very embarrassed when he actually replied. On the other side of the barrier was Jogbani. Here a similar pole; the driver woke a customs official only to be told that the officer in charge was away and anyway there was no need to report. So we were in India. I was too sleepy to notice much in the remainder of the journey. I remember we stopped to give the driver a rest, and I took James for a walk. The poor little fellow, barely awake, took one step and fell flat on his face on the tarmac. Too late I remembered that I had given him Vallergan to help him sleep through the journey! Sorry James.

As dawn broke, we found Northern India very like Nepal; good flat agricultural land. There was still plenty of water about, even though it was the beginning of April and there had been no rain for many months. Although Bihar State, it is in the south where is the drought and famine. We arrived early at Katihar at 5 am, because of the minimal delays at the checkpoints.

Though the Indo-Pakistan confrontation had been fought two years earlier, in 1965, there was still military activity on the road. However, I saw little in the way of actual weapons, spotting only three ton trucks, jeeps and motor-cyclists.

The train was scheduled a fifteen minute stop. While waiting, we sent Doma and James off on a tricycle-rickshaw ride round the station area to keep the little fellow entertained.

116

Swarming flies were a revolting sight. The whole canvas back of the landrover was a mass of moving entomology. One source was a dying woman, huddled in the most filthy rags imaginable, lying under the steps of the bridge that leads over the six railway lines. She stank of excreta and urine. We had been spoilt at the cantonment by the high standard of hygiene. The filth and squalor of the third-class waiting-room was a nasty reminder of what parts of India can be like.

Corruption is wide-spread, no less on her railways. The train duly arrived but I couldn't find the seats we had booked and the guards showed not the slightest interest in us or our requests for help. It was not, in fact, until I had pressed a ten-rupee note in an official's hand that our seats suddenly materialised. We were taken to our compartment which had its own lavatory. There was, of course, no paper and the wash-basin had those infuriating taps that you have to keep pressing to get any water. As there was no plug, the problems of a proper wash were quite considerable. There was, surprisingly, a shower. At least this was working, even though the lavatory seat was sprayed at the same time.

A young Indian doctor was also travelling in this four-berth six-seater carriage. He had obviously tipped the conductor to keep the compartment to himself, and we had only managed to get our seats because we had probably tipped more. He had, most grudgingly, allowed us into the carriage, where he was to spend the whole journey sprawled in his pyjamas, occupying three seats, while my party were crammed in the remaining three. It was interesting to note that these first class carriages can be locked from the inside to prevent anyone getting in. I had given James another dose of Vallergan and he was now fast asleep, stretched out across the back of our seats. He was a tall fourteen-month-old toddler and we were to have an uncomfortable journey, perched on the edge of ours.

No sooner had we taken our places than in came the sweeper. Thick dust rose from the filthy floor, as he stirred up the dirt with the brush which, like most in India, was a collection of twigs tied together. We made a hurried dash into the "fresh" air of the station. No sooner had we alighted than we were harassed by beggars. I have never come across such persistent and irritating begging anywhere in the world, as I did in India. One unfortunate man had suffered from polio and, as a result, his legs were thin, wasted and partially paralysed. He couldn't move except on all fours and protected his knees with rubber pads that had been cut from the circumference of a motor tyre. With his hands he held lumps of wood shaped like old-fashioned weights. At the same time he clutched a mug for coins.

At first we managed to keep the carriage cool with the aid of the four fans set in the roof but soon it became oppressively hot.

Eventually we reached Siliguri where John Masters' novel, "Bhwani Junction", was filmed. The porters carried our cases on their heads to the waiting taxi while I exchanged warrants for the return journey. It was then that I met with another European, who told me that I should have travelled "air-conditioned first-class", for there were such luxuries as sheets, soap and towels!

Before we could leave the station, we had to get permission to enter Darjeeling, being very near the Pakistan border. We completed detailed application forms and had our names checked carefully against the prohibited entry list. I noticed that this already contained a number of British names, the majority of which had "student" written against them! A nun had been waiting one and a half hours for the official to return from lunch to get her permit. We were luckier and were on our way, a little less than an hour after the train had arrived. There was a check-point two miles along the road, where we were delayed ten minutes while our papers were scrutinised. I took this opportunity to photograph a little train that zig-zags up the side of the mountain from Siliguri at 500 feet to well over 7,000 feet at Darjeeling. The train always has right of way. Otherwise the priority belongs to the ascending vehicle, which seemed to give my driver the right to overtake on blind bends and drive straight at oncoming vehicles! During the short descent into Darjeeling, he conveniently forgot this and continued down the middle of the road, blasting continuously on his horn.

The journey up from Siliguri had been most interesting. We passed through dense forest, home to the Bengal tigers, which are very occasionally seen on the road. Nearer the summit, we passed gardens, cut out of the steep mountainside; little streams trickled down between the rocks amongst them.

We left Doma at Ghoom, some five miles from Darjeeling, where she was to stay with her sister whom normally she but saw once a year, during Dashera. This was a bonus year with two visits! The journey from Katihar took two and a half hours and cost £2.50. We couldn't drive right up to the hotel, as no actual road led to it. I gave the driver a 25p tip, for which he appeared most grateful. This was more than the average day's wage for an employee in India.

We were met, just below the hotel, by three porters with the kindest faces I have ever seen. They carried our cases on their backs with the aid of a thin forehead strap to the ground-floor suite I had especially requested, as James had never seen a staircase. We didn't want our holiday marred by the worry of his falling down stairs. Everything was perfect, only the fuse-box and meter switch were "conveniently" placed two feet from the ground!

The room was decorated throughout in blue, a curtain dividing a sofa, a couple of arm-chairs and a desk, from the bedroom. Off the sitting-room was a spacious bathroom, ideal to dry the baby's napkins, only at seven thousand feet, it was far too cold to dry anything inside.

We were very grateful for the tea and cakes which arrived within minutes of our arrival. I felt even more content as I wallowed in a steaming bath and washed the soot from the train, out of my hair. I didn't know at the time there was a severe water shortage, resulting in power being was so low that the light from a candle was superior to a bulb. In addition, when the electric fire was switched on, there was insufficient current to see a glow. Early to bed was the rule.

Anna had felt very sick during the twisting journey up the mountain. The cold didn't help. As we sat in the drawing room, enjoying the blazing fire, I poured her the contents of a tin of mango juice and she soon felt better. It was there that I tasted my first Indian beer for a year; a quart bottle cost 40p. It tasted rather insipid and contained little alcohol, yet by the end of the week I had become very fond of it. After the meal, I spoke to the Tibetan girl who was daughter of the manager. I asked her why the plants were all covered with sacking. She explained that it had snowed heavily two weeks earlier, and hail and frost were expected any moment. In spite of the cold, I sat outside for half an hour gazing up at the sky. I had never seen so many stars.

That first night in Darjeeling was bitterly cold. Though given hot-water-bottles and plenty of blankets, this was still not enough. The curtains were so thin that James woke at the crack of dawn. I never dared tell Anna was that I found the most enormous spider I had ever seen in the bedroom.

I had to put on socks, a jersey over my pyjama top and my overcoat across the bed to eventually fall asleep hugging the hot-water-bottle. I was awakened a little before 5 o'clock by James and the night watchman. I hurriedly dressed over my pyjamas. I was not going to strip in that cold! I slipped on my overcoat and walked the quarter mile to Observatory Hill. In the few minutes it had taken to find my cameras, the room had become appreciably lighter. I thought, erroneously, I must have missed the sunrise. It was disappointing compared with the view from the Sanguri chalet the previous November. Even so, the mountains were very beautiful.

After breakfast, the first essential was warm clothes for James. We saw a delightful white rabbit-skin coat, just a shade too small. News of what we were seeking flashed through the bazaar. Within minutes, a trader ran out and James was fitted perfectly in a similar brown garment. He looked most charming. We visited Keventer's milkbar. On the roof, was a verandah where we sat. When the clouds cleared, the Himalayas were a magnificent sight. It is difficult to describe the pleasure a simple milkshake gave us. It was our first cow's milk in twelve months and quite delicious. We had tried buffalo milk before going back to powdered milk. We watched, amused, as James chewed his way through a number of straws; he couldn't get the hang of them at first.

We walked the two miles to the Himalayan Mountaineering Institute. On the way we passed under huge flowering rhododendron, in beautiful blood red blossom, others in white and pink. Some had reached 20 to 40 metres. We also passed bamboo, 15 metres high, some with a 6 inch diameter. These are used for bridge construction. Daisies grew out from vertical rock formations with stems at least twelve inches long.

CHAPTER 19

The Himalayan Mountaineering Institute

We passed through the zoological park, perhaps the highest in the world, stocked with indigenous birds and animals. The exception was a pair of Siberian tigers which had been presented by Khruschev some years earlier. They originated from Ussuri, later the site of the Russian-China border clash in 1969. Enormous by any standard, they were also so fertile that a very large number have been born. What impressed us was how the zoo had tried to reproduce as natural a setting as possible. There were plenty of trees in the extensive acreage in which the tigers were free to roam, with abundant foliage under which they could shelter during the heat of the day. We watched three large cubs play together and next the mother racing up the hill. After which she lay stretched out amongst the bushes, dozing in the sun. The tigers still had their winter coats, and looked healthier than any I have seen elsewhere.

It was good to see barking deer, as I had become very fond of these since James had played so contentedly with one in Lt. Colonel Shakespear's garden. It had been found in the forest and given to Gordon, to be tethered on his lawn. Although terrified of humans, it was perfectly happy to let James crawl over to play and even tolerate his attempts to poke it in the eye. Some workmen nearby, seeing I had a camera, tried to attract the deer by whistling and shouting. They even cut branches full of leaves and threw them over the fence, hoping to entice the animals. However the herd kept to a far corner until I barked like a dog when they trotted up with interest.

There were also red pandas (*ailurus fulgens*). Anna and I had first spotted one in the hills near Dharan. It had been a most unusual sighting as normally they are rarely found below seven thousand feet and are mainly nocturnal.

I originally wrote this chapter on Tuesday, September 3rd, 1968, and in one of the national papers that day I read the following short paragraph from the front page: *"Panda Captured"* *"Police and London Zoo officials this morning captured one of the two pandas which escaped on Sunday. Suka, a three year old Nepalese panda, was found in a dustbin near Chalk Farm Underground Station. Her mate, Rama, also three and about the size of a corgi is still missing. Officials warn the public not to try and pick him up".*

There was an oriental small-clawed otter, with a most attractive skin. They have unusual hand-like front paws ideal for foraging. We often spotted these on our walks around the camp. Amongst the hundreds of birds I had seen in the jungles of Nepal, none looked as lovely as the pheasants. The male plumage consisted of a blue neck and a rusty-coloured breast flecked with white feathers.

Tenzing Norgay, who scaled Mount Everest with Sir Edmund Hilary, was Director of Field Training at the Mountaineering Institute. We were unlucky that he was away that morning, though several of my colleagues had met him. He spoke excellent English and was not the least spoilt by his fame. We saw a piece of rock that had been taken from the summit and the clothing and equipment used for the ascent. The scale of rations required per man each day was demonstrated. There is, in addition, a powerful telescope for viewing Kanchenjunga and other great peaks which make such a beautiful background to Darjeeling.

I spent part of the following day obtaining permits to Senchal Lake and Kalimpong. They were so surprised at the Municipality that I should even wish to visit the lake, that at first they couldn't even find the book of permits. Ours cost

2½p. I went to the Foreigners' Registration Office in order to write a letter to the Superintendent of Police to request entry to Kalimpong.

I came across one of the very few references to the Abominable Snowman in my two years in the mountain kingdom, on a postage stamp of Bhutan State!

That afternoon, we set out for the Tibetan Refugees Self-Help Centre. Our hotel, the Windamere, was built at practically the highest point in Darjeeling, so to reach the Centre meant a pretty steep half-an-hour's climb down, made even more exhausting by taking an old push-chair for James.

The altitude affects the colour of the people. All have a ruddy complexion, tinged with blue. It was the same with the refugees in this camp. They seemed delightfully content with their lot; the children and mothers smiled broadly as we approached. All were dark haired and therefore intrigued by James with his fair skin and blond hair. This extraordinary fascination followed throughout the whole of the East and later in Africa. The local people couldn't resist touching him. James hated this and squirmed away in a most embarrassing manner. He played happily with any child of five or more but seemed bored by children of his own age. Perhaps, as they were physically so much smaller, he considered them too young.

We bought him a yak-wool sweater and sandals for Anna. Our guide took us to the kitchens which were immaculate and where, every day, food for four hundred adults is prepared, with as high a protein content as they can afford. The children were either playing or resting in row upon row of cots. They were looked after by half a dozen Tibetan woman. It was certainly most efficient and indeed they all looked very happy, but I wondered how much they missed the individual attention of their mothers.

As we climbed back to our hotel, we had a clear view of Lebong racecourse. This had been built about five miles from Darjeeling and could be one of the smallest and highest in the world. Racing ponies are all hill bred.

The following day we visited Senchal Lake, a reservoir, from which filtered water is supplied to Darjeeling from some six miles. This has been constructed in the game reserve, a most beautiful sylvan setting: the surroundings so peaceful that, although we spent the whole morning there, we met no one. The green of the forest was relieved by the red and pink blossom of enormous rhododendron and magnolia. Little paths ran through the forest until they petered out as the foliage grew too dense. It was then I became anxious in case we got lost. In addition, the knowledge that a Bengal tiger might be lurking behind a thicket added a certain apprehension.

At the dairy-farm at Ghoom, we met the sixty-four-year-old European manger, (most embittered he was with India and her politics and absolutely delighted to see us). His farm was now State owned. He took us first to his cows, most of which he kept inside a byre. Although they looked healthy enough, he complained that not only were they too small but their milk production less than half what it should be, due to far too much inbreeding. He had a superb bull who, though getting rather long in the tooth, had sired most of the herd. Apparently the bull's son was next door siring his great granddaughters! Because of severe currency restrictions, they could not import new blood and therefore unable to procure a second quality bull and after years of frustration, the farmer had lost interest in the cattle. His main joy was his pigs. These were of European stock and enormous. They were immaculately clean, as was the whole farm. The manager named them after film-stars and proudly introduced: James Mason, Marilyn Monroe and Doris Day. James loved them, especially the piglets. Bacon,

126

sausages and hams were all prepared at the farm. Most of the sausages and hams were sent to Calcutta. A few years earlier, he had sold pigs to the resettlement farm at Dharan, where they were successfully crossbred with the local wild variety. All were born infested with roundworms and had to be treated several times throughout their lives. They could very easily succumb to pneumonia, catching a chill after lying out in the sun, for the pigsties were very cold at night. The main worry however was swine fever which kills rapidly following high temperature and diarrhoea. Swine pox was also a constant threat. There was a certain amount of "foot and mouth", but as there were no laws demanding slaughter, the herds were protected by inoculation.

The recent devaluation of the Indian rupee had serious financial implications for our host, resulting in a heart attack from which he had only just recovered. He looked gaunt and ill. I later heard, from Doma's sister, that he had died only a few months later.

At one time Keventner's supplied the Windamere with milk, cheese and meat, but after some disagreement, this sadly was no longer so. The farm did supply the New Elgen hotel, about a hundred yards from our hotel. The cuisine might have been better but there was no running hot water! In all, the best place was the Planters' club, which one could join for 5p a day. There were less than ten permanent British residents in Darjeeling.

We left the sad farmer for Ghoom Monastery, the oldest in Darjeeling. On the way we were entertained by Tibetan women as they picked fleas from each other's heads, while sitting by the side of the road. Two monks, dressed in their long crimson robes, took us round the monastery, pointing out holy candles, prayer-wheels, turned by flames from the candles, and the many holy books. Outside, on the monastery

127

wall, were more prayer-wheels; these the monks turned by hand. The monks posed outside the monastery with their horns, at least twelve feet long. A blast emitted a deep boom echoing across the valley and terrifying James!

We set off for Kalimpong. The thirty-two miles, though fascinating, were too frightening to enjoy, with so many hairpin bends. We passed a miniature Buddhist temple, and after an hour, arrived at Observation Point, high above the meeting of two enormous rivers. A crystal-clear tributary joined a much larger dirtier river to form the Testa. The states of Sikkim, Bhutan and North Bengal were separated by these waters. Over to the East, we could make out the heavily-guarded Testa Bridge over which we would soon cross on our way to Kalimpong. The view from the hill was one of the finest we had had in India. It made a delightful resting-place. At the check-point, just before the bridge, we were handed a very dirty scruffy piece of paper, about the size of a postage stamp. This was our pass to cross the bridge! There was a lot of military activity and we passed several convoys of Indian troops as we approached the Chinese border.

Kalimpong was infinitely cleaner than Darjeeling. There were proper shops selling sophisticated items such as text-books and radios. We managed to buy a pair of red sandals for James. (Only later we found that red polish was quite unobtainable in India!)

We enjoyed a picnic lunch in the grounds of a deserted Scottish church. From there we climbed to the little Mission Hospital, beautifully situated overlooking the mountains. The local climate was delightfully cool at 2,500 feet. After Dr. Douglas, the Senior Medical Officer, had finished her work and lunch, we paid her a visit. I was particularly interested in the little hospital as many of our nurses had done all or part of their training here. Our Matron had earlier sent the doctor a gift of baby food. We discussed local folklore and local beliefs. She told us how, when pregnancy was delayed, the villagers unlocked everything in the house; also how they studiously avoided oranges when they had a cold!

The journey back to Darjeeling was worrying in that the car had developed a serious water leak. I was relieved that we had to re-cross the Testa because we needed water to refill the leaking tank. The oil and water heating lights came on again after a few more miles, although this did not concern the driver in the least. He explained how he had a spare gallon in the boot for a real emergency. Anyhow "he knew his car better than I did" and climbed a further three thousand feet with the red warning lights shining all the time. The driver reminded me he sometimes made the journey four times in a week!

On our last day in Darjeeling, we went to visit George Douglas who has illustrated this book and whose enthusiasm helped me complete my first. We collected fresh ham, cheese, butter and pork sausages from Keventer's. That afternoon we climbed Observatory Hill above the hotel. Every few steps along the narrow path sat beggars, waiting not only for the generosity of tourists but for alms from devout Buddhists, who had worshiped in the temple. There were many prayer flags around the Tibetan shrine. Anna likened these to hundreds of lines of washing. It was a beautiful, warm, sunny day, with hardly a cloud in the sky and the fluttering flags looked picturesque against the azure background.

We had another early start for our journey home, rising at 3.30 for a 4 a.m. departure. A landrover took us up a winding road to Tiger Hill, situated at an altitude of 8,482 feet, about seven miles from the Windamere. As we approached the peak, the light from the rising sun slowly illuminated the surrounds. The climb was very steep indeed. We reached the summit before dawn. It was bitterly cold. We took up our position, hiding James in Anna's coat, while we all three shivered. As the sun began to rise, all the colours of the rainbow appeared in bands across the horizon; these slowly gave way to first pink and then yellow. There was too much haze, so the actual sunrise was unduly prolonged. We could just visualise the Himalayan range by 5.15. Afraid we might miss the train, and with Anna and James chilled to the bone, we left. By way of compensation, we passed many glorious magnolia, their pink blossom picked out by the rising sun. Our car was ready at Ghoom, with Doma and her sister patiently waiting. We had a hair-raising return to Siliguri, as the driver free-wheeled most of the way, ignoring the rule to give way to ascending traffic. We arrived at the station with thirty-five minutes to spare.

Again we had trouble finding our seats in a train packed with soldiers. We breakfasted and lunched on packed meals provided by the Windamere kitchens, far more generous than their dinners. We arrived at Katihar at 2 p.m., the hottest time of the day and found, what we had most dreaded: no waiting transport. For an hour I haggled with taxi drivers before finding one prepared to take us to the border for £5. He drove fast and furiously until the car could take no more. About forty miles from Katihar, the engine made a sickening noise, smoke billowed out from under the bonnet and we shuddered to a halt. Fortune now favoured us. A few minutes later, our missing landrover appeared, a mere five-and-a-half hours late! Apparently air had blocked the fuel pipe and, not knowing what to do, the driver had simply sat by the side of the road until, hours later, a passing lorry-driver helped remedy the fault.

Now we were safely aboard, I could enjoy the journey once more. I noticed how cows, goats and even a young elephant had all been sprayed with red dye at the *Holi* festivities, held weeks before.

At the check point, the Customs Officer was furious that he had not been woken, to stamp our passports a week earlier. At one time it seemed we would not be allowed to leave India. Finally he relented, once I confided that I was the surgeon at the British Military Hospital. The day ended happily enjoying Keventner's pork chops.

CHAPTER 20

Rhinoceros

<u>Bhag</u> (leopard) with paw on shepherd's head.

Seventy-five miles south-west of Kathmandu is the little airstrip of Meghauli, situated on the border of King Mahendra's game reserve, some five miles from Tiger Tops, an ideal location from where to see the wild life of Nepal.

Tiger Tops is open all year round and April is perhaps the best month to view game. The vegetation is not too luxuriant as the monsoon has yet to break. The temperature and humidity are comfortable. The scenery is most beautiful from October to March, when the climate is delightful. Three of the world's highest peaks, but sadly not Mount Everest, can be seen from the hotel. During the monsoon, the journey from the airstrip is by boat, as the rivers are too deep to ford. The Ganges River dolphin can occasionally be seen in the water.

I left Gaucher airport at 7.30 a.m., on a chartered flight with eight round-the-world tourists. We arrived at the edge of the jungle. A crowd of villagers appeared as if from nowhere. They were fascinated by the plane, fingered the wings and gaped inside until chased away by the Captain. We passed the time photographing them until a landrover arrived, to be followed by two others ferrying guests back from their stay in the reserve. Each vehicle had an armed warden sitting on the bonnet, ready to deal with any charging game. They had just encountered rhinoceros and the tail end of a tiger.

I met Tiger Tops' managing director John Coapman, a huge man, son of two missionaries and a professional hunter. We climbed into the landrovers and drove a short distance into the jungle where we were met by five elephants – a tusker and four cows. The tusker, who was twenty-seven, was much the biggest. The tips of his tusks had been sawn off, as they had begun to split, for had this continued up to the gum, infection might have entered and the tusk lost. Only males have tusks. All five had been captured in Assam (N.E. India) in their early "teens" and had taken ten years to train. An elephant has three attendants who remain with it through life, even if sold. I was told that each understand about forty words of command. The team consists of an elephant driver, called the paneet in Nepal, (the mahout in India), the pachwa, who stands on the back, helping to direct and acting as look-out, and the cleaner who is actually called the mahout in Nepal and looks after the elephant when it returns from the jungle. All are respected because of the association of the elephant to the god Ganesh.

In 1967 a male elephant cost £400 and a female £500, but a further £700 a year to keep. One reason males are cheaper is that they are more difficult to control. A male, on maturity, is liable to periods of excitement known as being musth; these tend to occur in his late twenties and last ten days to two months. During this period he is unmanageable, even if provided with a partner. By drastically reducing his diet and working him very hard, his sexual potency should wane; otherwise he has to be chained up.

No mating is permitted, for the gestation is twenty to twenty-two months and the baby stays with its mother for twelve years. The young, being undisciplined, would soon wreck the hotel. Baby elephants are also difficult to rear. They tend to stand too long and therefore prone to swollen legs, which can become infected leading to septicaemia and death. This does not happen in the wild, when they are always on the move.

We mounted the elephants who were first made to kneel. We stepped on this leg, then on the tail, held across by the paneet, and finally swung ourselves over the rails of the howdah. On my elephant, which I had to myself, this was like a miniature four-poster canvas "bed", with ropes slung between posts about nine inches high. I sat cross legged, clinging to the ropes, and felt very comfortable.

We had hardly entered the jungle before disturbing spotted deer and peafowl. We spread out in extended line but saw little except the recent pug mark of a tiger. There are about three hundred in the neighbourhood. The prints of rhinoceros were pointed out to us. A herd of some fifty spotted deer raced away, sending up jungle fowl, from whom all domestic fowl descend.

After crossing five rivers, I spotted Tiger Tops, built on the banks of yet another tributary of the Rapti. The hotel consisted of a cluster of buildings, the two largest being on twenty-feet wooden stilts. These were the bedrooms, built thus for maximum ventilation, being high above the undergrowth. The stilts also provide protection from snakes and wild animals; keep the rooms dry during the monsoon flooding of the river, and provide a spectacular panoramic view of the Himalayas.

The elephants' heads passed under the verandah and it was easy to climb from the howdah up the three steps to the balcony; my bedroom being immediately opposite.

The set-up was magnificent. One building was actually built round an enormous tree. The wooden stilts had been sunk six feet in concrete. The second building was set back amongst the trees.

The circular dining-room was both spacious and cool; with a high roof, thatched on top of bamboo. The floor was built on three feet of sand, on top of which stones from the river-bed had been cemented in place. This made the floor slightly mobile – though I was hardly aware of this. This type of building is apparently safer where there could be earthquakes *(as happened in 1988, see epilogue)*. The fireplace was round, set on an eighteen-inch base. There was no chimney, just a hole for the smoke to escape through the high roof, thus sterilising the timbers.

TIGER TOPS

137

I had one of the twelve double bedrooms to myself. The gaps in the single plank floor meant that, after the lady above had powdered herself, there was a pile of the same on my bedside locker! The walls, constructed of bamboo canes, were so thin that I heard every sound, and the light of a hurricane lamp was clearly visible. There was no key ("no security needed as everyone is honest"), wire-netting for glass.

For lunch we had soup, spaghetti bolognese with sliced cabbage and carrot salad, pear jelly and cream, followed by coffee. This homely meal proved most popular. Fresh vegetables are grown in the vegetable garden and near-by village.

After lunch and an hour's rest, we were called around 5 p.m to climb back on to the elephants, reached from my balcony. Almost at once we saw jungle fowl and a langur monkey - large and grey, with black face and four-foot-long tail. We passed a couple of <u>machans</u>, (hides). Young buffalo are tied to stakes, thirty yards from these, every night between 6 p.m. and 9. p.m., in the hope that a tiger or leopard will make a kill. If they do, a warden will race back and the guests pile into landrovers and drive to the hide. There is no dressing for dinner!

The animal is observed for a short period with the aid of powerful spotlights. The tigers are fully aware of the human presence, snarling up at the lights while they feed. Tigers are much cleaner in that they will bury the intestines before tackling the carcase, thus postponing the arrival of vultures. They will neither eat meat touched by these scavengers nor return to a kill after forty-eight hours. Leopards are much dirtier. They soon foul up the meat by starting at the anus and gnawing their way through the carcase.

We passed a large pile of bones near one <u>machan</u>, the results of kills. These had been picked dry by jackals and vultures. The grass was burning. Fires, started in India, had spread up to the reserve. Every few seconds there was a sound like a pistol shot – the heat causing gas to expand inside the bamboo, which then exploded. This kept predators away from the vicinity of <u>machans,</u> a relief, as the buffalo trap seemed too cruel.

We were soon ploughing through elephant grass six to twelve feet above my head. I spotted a grey mound twenty yards in front as the huge Greater One-horned rhinoceros trampled through the grass. These can weigh 4,000kg. I leapt to my feet to film just as the <u>paneet</u> had urged his mount to give chase. Caught completely off balance, I crashed back, grabbing a supporting rope. We saw her three calves, lost track of the mother but disturbed barking and a hog deer. The excitement was immense. A <u>paneet</u> spotted a second and again we gave chase in extended line. We entered a river and there, just fifty yards away, was the rhino, its back to us. I felt perfectly safe as the rhino slowly waded through the shallow water. "Rhino!" shouted my paneet to summon the others. Hearing the shout, the rhino turned, snorted and charged through the shallow water. I wasn't frightened as the rhino looked much smaller through the view-finder, that I was able to film the whole scene until she stopped within twenty yards, deterred by the arrival of the other elephants. She veered off up a bank, to disappear in the tall grass; it had made glorious viewing. We returned to base at dusk for tins of Japanese beer, chilled in the kerosene fridge. Most drinks were available but expensive – with import duty and freightage.

After dinner, when pitch black, I sat in the back of an open landrover. Soon we saw three sets of eyes glowing in the distance. Approaching these, we found ourselves amongst spotted deer; so close that we could have touched them. Most animals are mesmerised by light. As we explored further, we saw barking and hog deer. The previous night a leopard had crossed in front of the landrover, just four hundred yards from the hotel. The hills were beautiful from the glow of forest fires. Suddenly we smelt that powerful, obnoxious odour of tiger. We waited and waited but to no avail.

CHAPTER 21

Tiger

I was up at 6 am filming the reflection of sunrise on the Rapti; an unforgettable memory, the red light filtering through the forest trees. Reveille was at 6.30 and after coffee and biscuits, we explored a most attractive valley, with high banks, topped by huge trees. We followed this until the leading elephant sank so deeply into the river that the water reached practically eye level.

This is a favourite haunt of the rhino, but being so narrow, it is dangerous to meet them there. We spotted a number of attractive kingfishers and a very large eagle.

About a mile and a half from camp, the more weary members of our group (the average age must have been nearly seventy) – left to go back by landrover, while the rest of us returned to the marshy ground. It felt like being on a ship as we rolled our way through grasses, like huge waves above us. Soon we came across definite tracks and flattened areas where the rhinoceros rest. In some were large heaps of excreta. Rhino are creatures of habit. They prefer to defaecate at the same spot, into which they back. Poachers are well aware of this and may hide two or three days, for the opportune moment to explode their muzzle in the rhino's ear. In the four months prior to my visit, five had been slaughtered but six born. The traffickers are dealt with "very seriously" by the game wardens.

Rhino, in Nepal, are the third rarest in the world – after those of Java and Sumatra. They are in great danger of extinction. In the orient, the rhino's horn is thought to have a potent aphrodisiac effect and its black market value varies from £300 in Calcutta to £600 in Hong Kong.

I was feeling rather peckish, after our early start, and with the sun well up, held little hope of spotting further game when the peace was shattered by my paneet shouting "Rhino!" and there, fifty yards ahead, the grass was waving. We gave chase in extended line but too far apart, and the rhino – unseen by me but spotted by the paneet – had doubled back between us. We found her again, broadside on, seventy yards back. We closed slowly to within fifty to discover that she had a baby with her. She turned and charged.

I snapped her quickly before the terrified paneet turned the elephant and fled. The rhino stopped. We turned again. She charged a second time. By now we had been joined by the tusker and a second elephant. The two who had bolted furthest at the initial charge, had been rounded up and were just behind.

The paneets were yelling, while the elephants were trumpeting and trembling with fury. Faced by this solid wall of elephant, the rhino stopped, a mere ten yards from us and trotted off, followed by the calf she had left behind. We last saw her two hundred yards away, on the opposite side of a river.

Two weeks earlier, a rhino had charged one of the cow elephants which had turned to face the assault. An elephant cannot normally be concussed, having a seventeen-inch, honeycombed skull which will absorb practically any blow. What this elephant didn't know was the second rhino behind which also charged, striking a vicious blow on her left flank.

A rhino can kill an elephant, for the latter's hide is comparatively thin. If the rhino gets his horn under the elephant's belly, he can eviscerate the animal. A fortnight after I left Tiger Tops, the tusker had a lucky escape when a charging rhino ripped open his side. A lady tourist was so terrified that she leapt off the howdah but by some miracle escaped unharmed.

143

Rhino's hide was used for war shields, yet the elephant's hide is so thin that a bite from a horse-fly will cause it to bleed. I was relieved to learn the elephant's skull was so thick, because I was distressed by how savagely the <u>paneets</u> beat their charges using a sharp iron rod called an *ancus*. The slightest stumble, disobedience or slowness to respond is rewarded by a vicious blow which would kill a man.

We returned for a welcome breakfast, before taking a landrover to a stretch of water to observe a couple of mugger crocodiles (*crocodylus palustris*) basking in the sun. A duck swam past while a snake-catcher was fishing close to, yet were ignored. It was too late in the day for activity. This peace and tranquillity can be deceptive. A year earlier, a woman had been collecting water from this very spot, when she had been swept into the water by the crocodile's tail. She was never seen again.

Accidents are not uncommon at Tiger Tops. A man had been knocked into the river in front of the hotel during the monsoon, when he had been hit by a half-submerged log; his friend had leapt to his rescue. Neither were seen again.

Rhinos also reap vengeance. A villager carrying firewood had been caught from behind, as was one of the game wardens. Even visitors are at risk. A man stepped off the balcony while photographing his friend mounting an elephant. He was unconscious for two hours with a fractured skull. A lady tourist sustained a fractured kneecap due to a fall from an elephant which she had only mounted to pose for a photograph!

There were a pair of man-eating tigers at Nawalpur, some twenty-six miles from Tiger Tops; their toll, at that time, was over fifty. The local aborigine neither burn nor bury their dead, and it is possible that these have developed a taste for human flesh because of availability, especially if there had been a shortage of, or problems killing, their natural prey. It is said that human flesh is comparatively tasteless. Herb Klein, one of John's partners, had gone after them two months earlier but with no success. John was also to try, even though outside the hunting season and the reserve. I later learned that he too was unsuccessful and the two tigers were still at large.

I took a walk at midday, as I wanted to examine the buffalo remains and photograph the <u>machans</u>. I was provided with a guide in return for treating the sick amongst the staff. He carried a double-barrelled shotgun. I was far more apprehensive of the gun than the prospect of meeting an animal; he seemed to have little discipline and I repeatedly found it pointing in my direction.

While away, I missed the elephants taking their bath in the river, having a wonderful time spraying each other, but saw many jungle fowl and found photography far easier than from the back of an elephant.

That evening, after three beers, hamburgers and walnut pudding – a great delicacy in the States – we set off to be amongst large herds of spotted deer with their magnificent antlers. We disturbed wild boar and gave chase, until they disappeared, as if by magic, into a small bush. A rhino was crashing through the undergrowth, just fifteen yards from the landrover. Bob turned the open landrover for a better view but now a rapid exit was impossible and, being so close to the ground, I was really worried and told him so. He simply laughed, but I pointed out that he was all right with me and a second tourist shielding him. By now we really were stuck, as the other landrover had drawn close behind. We couldn't even reverse!

I was given a different elephant, which I shared with a young American girl, on the final morning. A tiger had been calling, just over the river, for most of the night. We spotted several sets of tigers' marks in the sand by the water, and also impressions left by bear. After wading through the grasses for some twenty minutes, I heard the shout I had been waiting for so long: "Tiger"!

Oh, the frustration of being on the slowest elephant! A professional photographer had "mine". An elephant had disturbed three fully-grown tigers: a tigress with two grown-up cubs. They had broken cover from almost immediately under her.

There was so much shouting and excitement yet I saw nothing. Then at last, there she was, forty yards in front. Even at that distance, the tigress looked enormous and her markings truly beautiful. She glided through the tall grass with majestic ease. We gave chase. I tried desperately to film her, but with the elephant crashing through the grass, trembling and trumpeting, the paneet leaping up and down and my companion nearly pushing me under the ropes in her excitement, I could hardly get the view-finder to my eye, let alone film.

We closed to within twenty yards and for two glorious minutes chased her through the grass until she finally gave us the slip. I then noted that we were alone; the other four had pursued the cubs. We reluctantly accepted it was safer to give up the hunt. The tusker was very upset. Once he had been charged by a tiger and now, whenever he scents one, he is difficult to control – wanting revenge. The largest tiger killed in the vicinity – before the reserve was opened – was eleven feet two inches, nose to tail, four feet high and weighed over eight hundred pounds.

We watched the elephants returning from the jungle, piled high with grass, their staple diet. The paneets perched on their heads holding black umbrellas to protect themselves from the fierceness of the sun. The long grass was prepared in bundles which were rolled into large balls, after rice had been added, to feed the elephants, who weigh 4-5 tons and eat 150kg of vegetation a day.

At the <u>mahout's</u> command, the standing elephant lowered his head. The <u>mahout</u> placed a foot on one tusk and the other on the second, holding both as the elephant raised his head as a lift. When the elephant had reached the appropriate height, the <u>mahout</u> took three steps on to the elephant's head. He was sitting comfortably two seconds after standing on the ground!

As I signed the visitors book, I noticed how I was only the third Englishman to have visited Tiger Tops since it had opened in November 1965. Prince Philip, Henry Kissinger and Mick Jagger were all to follow "on my howdah" in future years.

This nearly all came to an end in September 2004. Maoist rebels demanded closure of the reserve in retaliation for the break down in talks with the Prime Minister. Prior to this they had already set off a bomb in the safari Kathmandu office and destroyed the control tower at the airstrip. I understand money probably changed hands and Tiger Tops reprieved.

BACK TO WORK

A cow herd – his Kukri tucked in <u>patuka</u> (cummerband).

CHAPTER 22

Kala-Azar

Kala-azar, or visceral leishmaniasis, has many other names including "black sickness", as it causes dark pigmentation of the skin, "sahib's disease", having a predilection for new arrivals to the Indian sub-continent and "Dumdum fever", being once so common in Calcutta, sharing its name with the airport. It was the cause of thirty-six-year-old Budhamaya's serious ill health and, indirectly, the loss of her two children.

The disease has been known to occur in serious epidemics along the Brahmaputra valley and as that river runs through Northern Assam, it was not surprising that the disease was common in Dharan as recently as 1964, with Nepal and India adjacent. After that, we saw very little of the disease, as many insect-borne diseases have been eradicated.

The villain of the piece is a tiny parasite, Leishmania donovani, named jointly after the co-discoverers of this protozoan, which is injected into the victim by a tiny insect, the sandfly Phlebotomus Argentipes.

Dharan was an ideal place for the disease to prosper, being a mere thousand feet above sea level, mainly rural with a high humidity during the monsoon, as many rivers flow nearby - perfect conditions for the sandfly. The human body does its best to contain the parasite, by taking it up in the spleen, liver and lymph nodes, but man cannot naturally kill the parasite and these organs subsequently enlarge enormously. Some parasites remain in the circulation so that other sandflies are infected, as they suck the diseased blood to pass on the disease.

Budhamaya had been ill six years but it was only when the disease had reached its terminal stages, that she had made the journey to Dharan. She came from a little village of Letang

Sansare - a journey which she would have done in six hours in her heyday, but now had taken two days by buffalo cart. Six years earlier she had suffered with a high fever that had taken over two weeks to abate. It had been during this that black patches of pigmentation had formed on her gums. Kala-azar had left its mark. Ever since, she was periodically drenched with soaking sweats.

During one such spell, she had been confined to bed and her five-year-old daughter dressed up in Budhamaya's sari. The little girl had been taking her mother a cup of tea, when the sari caught alight and the child so severely burned that she died four months later; she had never even been to hospital. During another incapacitating period, her little boy developed dysentery. She was unable to nurse him, being too weak herself. He also died. Yet another bout, two years before, had left her so moribund that she had lain comatosed with her lips apart. Flies had swarmed over her face; after a few days, maggots were actually crawling over her gums.

Matters had become critical four months before the buffalo cart brought her to us. Her abdomen had enlarged alarmingly, her liver was now cirrhotic; I guessed it was so damaged by the protozoan that it had begun to fail.

A friend advised that the best medicine was a large tot of hot rakshi; this she readily took, and protested that her distension had improved. However, following this, her condition had become so severe that, in spite of further rakshi, she could hardly breathe. (I later discovered that she had consumed vast quantities of this rum during these months). I felt her abdomen for the spleen, which should be enlarged. Because of her ascites, her tummy was as tight as a drum. It was impossible to feel any organ. I sent off a sample of blood; she was very anaemic, her white cells were reduced with the suggestive Napier's test positive in only twenty minutes; all this spelt Kala-azar. The disease was now chronic. As always, I was desperately short of beds, but two patients were due to go home in a couple of days.

"Come back then and I will find you a bed", I promised. Her face, pathetic at the best of times, looked even more miserable, if that were indeed possible.

"I'll give you two rupees", she said, "if you admit me".

"What if I don't?" I asked.

"I will spend them in Dharan until you can find me a bed", she sighed.

I performed a rough calculation in my mind. The hospital was costing £100,000 a year and this was excluding the cost of water and electricity which must have been considerable. There were seventy beds; that made the cost over £4 per day. She was offering me 10p for £8, and that if she only stayed two days.

Mike Banahan found her a bed and she was admitted that same afternoon. So ill was she, that she couldn't sleep. The ascites (fluid in her abdomen) had so pushed up her diaphragm that lying flat caused acute respiratory embarrassment. She spent the night in an armchair. Quick as a flash, one of the mothers, who was staying with her sick baby, leapt into the vacated bed.

We started Budhamaya off on antimony treatment and, for the first time in six years, she should have started on the slow road to recovery. She kept her two rupees to help with the expenses of going home.

Budhamaya, however, did not progress as quickly as she had expected and certainly, according to her, not as quickly as when she had "cured" herself with the rakshi. She had seen villagers come in, have their operations and go home, while she made little progress –not surprising considering how damaged was her liver.

She was terribly distressed. Even after Mike drained over twenty pints of fluid, her girth did not appear any less. This added to her misery. It was then, however, for the first time, that I could at least ballotte her enormous spleen which had extended six inches below the rib cage.

Finally, at the beginning of Dashera, her patience snapped. She wanted to go home to consult the witch doctor! The Sister found her wandering down the corridor, fully dressed, intent on leaving. After a long discussion with Mike, she reluctantly returned to her bed. Two days later, the same day as the *Mar* sacrifice, again she tried to leave. As usual, the ward was hectically busy, being run by a skeleton staff, so that as many as possible could attend the Dashera festivities. At that time we had in a little boy with Tetanus (lockjaw) requiring constant attention. The Sister couldn't cope with Budhamaya's antics. Incidentally, we had excellent results with tetanus patients, by immediate tracheostomy and administration of largactil.

"If she wants to go that much, let her go", I sighed.

She lived a distance away, so, out of the Villagers' fund, which we keep for emergencies such as these, we gave her twenty rupees for the bus-fare home. Her two rupees had multiplied by ten! It was then that Bulhamaya turned very sour, claiming that she had already deposited twenty rupees with the ward staff on arrival! We took her down town by ambulance, but there she flatly refused to board the bus towards her home. She was very crafty and made full use of the undeniable fact that she was extremely ill and in a pathetic state, by appealing to the crowd for having been so "hard done by" at the hospital! Being Dashera, everyone was in a jovial, good neighbourly mood. Her cause was soon taken up and she was carried to the police station by the protesting crowd. All afternoon anxious messages were relayed asking what the doctors should do. Finally we sent a spokesman down to explain to the police how it was she herself who had insisted on her discharge.

On my rounds next day, I was astonished to see Budhamaya. Somehow she had got back to bed, taken off her clothes and sat under the sheets, as if nothing had happened. Soon, however, she tired of this, and sat naked in a side room kept for orthopaedic equipment, between frames, weights and pulleys!

Next she appeared under her bed eating bhat (food) that she had bought in the town with our rupees, flatly refusing either to come out or co-operate in any way. Holiday or no holiday, this would not do! Everyone has their price, even at Dashera. Porters were quickly found and Budhamaya was soon despatched home, part by ambulance and the remainder on the backs of porters. There was a huge sigh of relief. Her offer of two rupees had turned out very expensive for the British Military Hospital.

At last it dawned that it was the withdrawal of the rakshi, while in hospital, that had resulted in this extraordinary behaviour. Soon, I knew, she would be back on alcohol, and with the rakshi would return her sanity and her last hope of recovery.

CHAPTER 23

Home Made Guns

The majority of poachers' shotguns were hand-made muzzleloaders. One of the most common methods of making such a gun was to procure, somehow or other, a pipe, as from beneath a wash basin. The pipe would be reinforced by wrapping wire round it. These illegal weapons, kept out of sight of any prowling policeman, were hidden mostly in the forest, to rust in the monsoon, when the wires weakened. The Nepalese, oblivious to danger, collected their guns and even if they hadn't been used for several months, loaded and fired.

Budhibahadur had one such gun, which even his grandfather had owned. He was in the jungle around half past three one afternoon, hunting jungle fowl, when the barrel exploded with disastrous results to both hand and gun, neither of which was recognisable as such. He had blown off his thumb, shattered the other fingers, damaged both the main arteries to his wrist and the main nerve, the median nerve. His hand was charred and blackened.

Somehow he was still alive when he arrived at the hospital and immediate resuscitation with blood, plasma and dextran improved his condition. He would not let us amputate his useless hand. I tried my best to save it although I had to sacrifice his index finger as it was dangling uselessly. I attempted to repair a hole in an artery but the wall was so friable that my sutures could not control the haemorrhage. I had to tie it, while removing charred and dead tissues.

He was very sorrowful. He admitted that it was all his fault: – he had been shooting in the closed season, when the animals have their young, and this was how the gods had punished him.

Next day there was no circulation to his fingers. But the following day, things looked a little brighter as some flow had returned and he could now move them just. But after another 24 hours, things seemed worse. The hand was swollen and he required a lot of morphia. His progress fluctuated over the following days althought he still had some movement. At this stage I was due to go on holiday but, just before I left, he asked me to take it off. I stupidly said we would wait a little longer.

The locum surgeon arrived and dressed the hand, now badly infected. He recommended amputation but Budhibahadur changed his mind yet again and decided to keep it. As a compromise, he finally agreed to watch while it was being dressed without an anaesthetic; it was a horrible sight – but still he wouldn't agree. To lose a hand is a terrible disaster anywhere in the world but perhaps an even greater one in a non welfare-state country like Nepal. Budhibahadur and his family might simply starve; if there was a chance, he must take it. Five days later the surgeon dressed his hand again but by now the middle finger was so rotten it had to come off.

Three days later Budhibahadur finally changed his mind and agreed – thirty long days after his admission. His hand was removed through the wrist and at last the wound healed, but the soldier was inconsolable.

I saw him several more times as an out patient, on my return and always he complained of <u>duca</u>, pain. He had been in hospital two months but, when he reported for his pay, was told that he could have nothing, as the injury was his own fault and had occurred after working hours!

Budhibahadur had been assisted during his period in hospital, in that the hospital provided his meals, but his wife had to borrow two hundred Nepalese rupees to exist, at the usual exorbinate rate of interest of 10 per cent per month.

Budhibahadur, at last, had a bit of luck – through the auspices of Brigadier Taggart, the Engineers created a job for him, pumping the bellows for the blacksmith, in the workshop of the Royal Engineers. At least he was getting some money. I advised him to pay back the loan as quickly as possible, but I doubt that he did and surmised that he would remain in ever-increasing debt, like so many others, for the rest of his life, and after that the debt would fall to his son.

THE FAR EAST

A Brahmin with namaste greeting

CHAPTER 24

Sanguri Châlet

Washing up with an unwelcome guest – a cobra.

We took our second holiday in November 1967 over a year and a half after we had first arrived in Nepal. It was 4 p.m. when I set off with nineteen-month-old James to Jogbani to pick up the relief surgeon arriving from Singapore. James loved the journey as the road was crowded with animals: cows, pigs, goats, buffalo and monkeys. We crossed the newly constructed East-West highway that will one day vastly improve communications throughout the whole country.

On this particular journey, I was not even asked to show my passport, as I crossed the border, to reach the railway station. I hadn't been there more than a few minutes before my surgical colleague arrived: exhausted, unshaven and looking filthy. He had been very shaken by his first experience of

India. The train journey, in the past twenty-four hours, had been unbelievably revolting. Without a young British subaltern, who spoke Nepalese. He feared he could never have made the journey. They were ordered out of their train in the middle of the night and had no idea to which of many platforms to go. In spite of being a doctor and knowing the risks, he had been so parched that he had actually bought an ice cream at one of the stations.

It was the night of the Diwali light festival and on our way back we saw candles in every abode. In some Tharu villages, a lantern had been hung high above the dwelling, slung on bamboo poles. Children had laid straw across the road and then set light to it, so we had to drive through walls of fire. In the fields, men and boys were waving burning sticks around like catherine-wheels.

My holiday officially began when I left home at 5 a.m. on November 3rd. A landrover arrived five minutes earlier and Narbahadur and I drove to Phusre Camp, where the old hospital had once been. The buildings had long since been handed over to the Nepalese Army, the local electricity and water boards. It was nearly dark as we started our climb and cold enough for pullovers. In the coolness of the morning, the ascent was infinitely easier than in the heat of the day. The distance seemed halved. We passed a notice, written in Nepalese, where engineers, who were constructing a water pipe-line to Dharan township, had tried to reassure local farmers that this would not affect the irrigation of their rice fields. The river was so low at this time of the year that we crossed by stepping from rock to rock. I puffed and blew my way up the mountain, while the young mali climbed effortlessly, carrying all the bags. We ascended 5,000 feet nearly non-stop. As the sun rose, I felt weary and sick. We stopped at the little village for tangerines: the sweetness again revived me and I was ready for the steepest part of the mountain, nicknamed the "chimney". Here I appreciated the little alpine rock plants that Anna had noticed on our last climb. Half an hour later, I caught my first glimpse that year of Everest. Immediately my legs felt lighter. However, the path had become very narrow and treacherous, being wet with dew and fallen away in parts. We had to watch our foot very carefully.

Soon I spotted the flat-roofed châlet and minutes later "collapsed" on to a wicker chair to admire the view, while Narbahadur busied himself in the kitchen heating the porridge that Anna had prepared the night before. I had missed the dramatic colours of dawn, yet the view of the mountains was crystal clear, with Everest dominating as ever. A gale must have been blowing over the great mountain as a huge snow cloud hurried off the peak. We could see the village of Dhankuta, down below, clearly from the châlet.

At half past eight, refreshed by breakfast, we literally ran down the slope back towards Dharan. Minutes later I paid for this folly as I slipped off the crumbling track and fell sprawling into bushes that fortunately were growing on the side of the mountain. These I clutched in desperation. I was covered in scratches and bruises. Narbahadur dragged me back. After this, I took things a great deal more carefully.

I had consumed a lot of coffee while admiring the mountain spectacle and nature finally made a stop imperative. To my horror I had chosen a rock a mere two feet from a large cobra. Luckily it was not the least interested in me! It slowly slid up the bank, to glide under the roots of a hollow tree. I kept my eyes skinned for ten minutes, until the snake moved a fraction and I was able to spot it. Narbahadur was most anxious the whole time. He warned me that it was very poisonous and begged me to keep further away. It was a relief to sip a very sweet cup of char, served at the little tea house, in the "tangerine" village.

CHAPTER 25

Hong Kong

"May you live in interesting times" – (old Chinese curse)

We chose Guy Fawkes day for the start of our holiday proper, setting off at 8 am for the airport, with Doma and her son Sorat. Fourteen miles down the road, the snow capped peaks looked very beautiful behind us. James explored the old Royal Nepalese Airlines dacota which was to take us to Dum Dum, before going back with Doma. Though Anna was sad at being parted from James for the first time, he went off happily, despite Rachel staying with us, and it was not until bedtime that he appeared to notice our absence. He was very comfortable with our neighbours, Gordon and Jean Shakespear (and Doma, of course!)

We arrived at Adi's house where, as music critic to the Calcutta Times, he had been given complimentary tickets to a "mod" German ballet in the New theatre. It was most enjoyable, being such a contrast to the tranquillity of home.

After the show, we drove to the German Consulate, where the male cast were already assembled. We were greeted by the German Ambassador, his charming wife and the many guests. Bowls of soup were dispensed before we climbed upstairs for a magnificent cold buffet. A huge salmon, beautifully prepared, was the centrepiece. I did full justice to this feast, washing it down with hock.

We were travelling to Hong Kong on a chartered Boeing 707, one of many flights ferrying Gurkha troops and their families between Dum Dum, Hong Kong and Singapore.

We were greeted by an Air India stewardess with a charming <u>namaste</u>. Another was so bored during the flight that she whisked Rachel away to play with her! There were over 150 passengers: Gurkha soldiers, wives and babies. At lunch, one of the women, sitting opposite, started writhing in agony. It is very difficult to perform an adequate examination on a plane, especially on Nepalese ladies who, whenever they have abdominal pain, bind yards of cloth round their middle. Hers was so tight that it must have caused severe cramp. She was fourteen weeks pregnant, very frightened at leaving home and terrified by the flight. I had some aspirin, so I prepared a solution which she took in a single gulp, before turning the little B.O.A.C. mug upside down, a custom the Nepalese have to show that the drink is finished.

To add to her fears, the plane started bumping and emitting weird noises. The engines seemed to roar, then cut out. I must admit that I too was pretty apprehensive but the woman was distraught. We later learned that we were flying on the edge of typhoon Emma. After what seemed an eternity, we started the descent. I tried my best to get the girl to swallow air and then suck a sweet to help relieve the pain that she was getting in her ears, but she would not or could not understand.

Minutes later I noticed the islands around Hong Kong. These I pointed out. This was a huge mistake, as she was now convinced she was going to die and only the strength of her husband, the assistance of a second Gurkha soldier and the safety belt, which I insisted that she had fastened, restrained her. The actual landing was reasonably smooth, but the noise of the reverse thrust was too much. She forced her arms above her and almost burst the strap as she cried, "Amah, amah". (Mother, Mother). Finally the plane came to a halt and the exhausted woman vomited into the air-sickness bag, totally shattered.

We were impressed at the airport to be met by a stewardess who provided a basket-cum-luggage-holder on wheels for

Rachel. The passport check took but a second and we started hunting for our luggage.

"I have bad news for you", a staff-sergeant expounded. "We have had a signal. Your cases, along with eight pieces of Gurkha baggage, have been left behind at Dum Dum"!

Next morning we set forth to collect our suitcases, but the typhoon was still blowing and grit kept getting in our eyes; it was also very wet. I ran to the Chinese Emporium and bought an umbrella, but in the gale, it was impossible to put up. Anna hid Rachel snugly under her coat. We crossed over on the ferry and took a bus to the airport to arrive long after the plane was due but there was no news of it. We impatiently watched a closed circuit television for announcements.

At the bar, we had sumptuous ham-and-egg sandwiches and found the waiter far better informed than the screen. He imparted that a plane had burst a tyre on the runway (that is built out into the sea), while taking off, and had crashed on to the water: miraculously only one passenger had been killed. The Pan American plane, with our cases, would have had to circle Hong Kong, for at least an hour, on the edge of the typhoon, whilst the runway was cleared. The pilot, wisely, flew on to Tokyo. Empty-handed and very despondent, we boarded a bus back to the Star ferry. We were most impressed when the conductor ordered two boys to give up their seats. Another had previously offered Anna his seat on the journey to the airport. The women were fascinated by our blonde headed baby.

Rachel settled immediately after her feed. Feeling rather guilty, we left her sleeping peacefully to hurry to a Parisian restaurant, just round the corner from the hotel. There we drowned our sorrows in Château Mouton Rothschild to accompany a succulent fillet steak. A tiny glass vase, with a solitary red rose, was the romantic centrepiece to our table.

The whole restaurant was tastefully decorated with Parisian scenes. The headwaiter spoke only French but so slowly and clearly that we could understand him. The only hitch was that Anna was still wearing the same dress and her footwear was flip-flops. We left immediately we had finished but, on rounding the corner, were horrified to see fire engines and police cars with flashing lights outside the hotel. We raced down the street, dodged past the officials and took the stairs four at a time. We burst into the bedroom and there was Rachel sleeping peacefully, exactly as we had left her. There had been an electrical fault with the lift and, because of the "Red Guards", any trouble was immediately reported to the authorities, in case of a bomb.

I had bought maroon pyjamas with matching dressing-gown at the Chinese Emporium. Anna looked stunning wearing just the pyjama top! The next essential was to fit her out with some decent clothes. She chose a turquoise wool skirt with a matching silk blouse which were, ironically, made in America. It was there we were told just how frequently they 'kitted out' airline passengers, whose luggage had been left behind: "It was almost as if they were in league with the airways"! Rachel was no problem, we had packed all her clothes in the carrycot. Shopping in Hong Kong was a joy, everything was so cheap. It was lovely to enter fabulous shops after the one and only bazaar in Dharan. Perhaps our most amusing purchase was a wig. The fitting was accompanied by giggles from the half dozen girl assistants as they tried various designs. Anna has naturally black hair yet she looked surprisingly beautiful in a honey coloured wig! It cost £5. Later this caused quite a stir in Dharan when, at a party, Anna overheard "Who is that?" At the jeweller's, Philip Chu, we bought two strands of semi-baroque pearls with a beautiful gold pearl clasp. The shop had been recommended by our

American friends, Ralph and Ruth, who had stayed three days with us the previous November, for a golf tournament.

When we returned to our hotel, there was a message that our suitcases had arrived. Everything improved from that exact moment. The weather cleared and the view during the ferry crossing was fabulous. I was sitting on a No.5 bus, like the red double-deckers at home, when a shattering explosion shook the bus from, perhaps, half a mile away. I read, next day, that the "Red Guards" had exploded a bomb; five had been killed with thirty-nine injured. (*In 1966, protests over an increase in the Star Ferry fares led to riots in Kowloon. In 1967 these flared up again as young followers of Mao besieged Government House. Disturbances continued throughout the summer, thousands of bombs were planted, killing fifteen, including children, and injuring many more. This had come to a climax during our short visit!*)

The flight back to Calcutta was to be most memorable. The crew chatted to us much of the time, as again we were the only ones they could readily converse with. I was invited into the cabin and given a seat behind the co-pilot. At the time we were flying along a twenty-five mile corridor across Vietnam. The pilot kept the radar beam straight down at 6 o'clock and explained that, so long as we did not deviate from this, we would not stray. We saw a number of planes in the air space and then an enormous fire on the ground. Almost certainly the U.S. Forces had been under heavy bombardment and had lit daylight flares. All civil planes were carefully monitored through the corridor by both sides. Our radar screen appeared so faint that we couldn't even pick up the aeroplanes we passed in the corridor! We were flying at 31,000 feet. The planes, I was told, were not equipped for high altitude, except for short periods. The U.S. bombers flew much higher, usually at 48,000 feet when the pilots need oxygen. Anna took my place in the cockpit and had the frightening experience of being hunted by two searchlights. The pilot pointed out Da Nang, later to be featured in Graham Greene's "The Quiet American".

The steaks we were given were over an inch thick and extremely tender. They were the most delicious we could ever remember. But soon we had to pay for this! The second pilot came up to enquire me if I was carrying any alcohol. I told him I wasn't, and he asked if I would take through the customs, half a bottle of brandy for each member of the crew. This I willingly agreed to.

The landing of the Boeing 707 at Dum Dum was perhaps the most exciting part of the flight. The runway was lit up by two rows of lights so that, from high up, it really looked very beautiful. As the plane was talked down, I sensed a certain tension in the cockpit. I wondered if the reason was the low oil pressure warning lights but I didn't like to ask!

We had a long wait for our cases. The crew and the air hostesses passed through quickly having no luggage. They kept hanging around for their brandy. It was really most embarrassing as I had planned to hand it over quietly outside. When our cases materialised, they were cleared at once. The "eager beaver" second pilot was on to us the moment we left the building, before we had even paid the porters.

Next day we took a car to Agra, but brother Brice commented: "a story too far".

ANNA, IN HER HONG KONG BLOUSE, WITH RACHEL

CHAPTER 26

Srinagar

It was an early start from Delhi to Kashmir. Anna was up at 4 a.m. to feed Rachel and it was a quarter to six when we were downstairs in the hotel lounge. The doorman whistled for a taxi. There were five in the courtyard but the drivers were all fast asleep in the back of their cabs. One of the floor boys banged on a roof and an extraordinary sack-like apparition appeared from the back. A head finally materialised and the car came over. The driver wanted three rupees for the five minutes journey to the airlines office. I gave him two, pointing to his broken meter.

A stewardess invited us into two seats in the front of the plane, with Rachel, in her basket, propped up on a pile of mail-bags. There were three stops on the way to Srinagar. We enjoyed our first proper meal since breakfast in Agra twenty-four hours earlier, making short work of fresh warm French rolls, hard-boiled eggs, apples and coffee; our only frustration being no time to finish, before the descent to Chandigarh. We had to fasten our safety belts and therefore surrender our trays. Photography was forbidden. I soon saw why. At least six fighter jets took off and there were many military helicopters about. The airport was a hive of activity. I was surprised that it was shared with civil airlines at all. Barbed wire fences were everywhere. The cold war was much in evidence.

During the second stage to Amritsar, the Himalayas became clearly visible. Glaciers were prominent. The next was Jammu, the winter capital. There we left Rachel in the care of two stewardesses. The runway was lined with a thin strip of metal rings. I guessed it was also very short by the way the plane revved up before taking off. As we approached the valley of Srinagar, we were flying at only 10,500 feet. Snow-capped mountains towered above us. We passed row upon row of razor-sharp rocks covered by thick and extensive forest. Rivers meandered through steep gorges, and here and there we spotted the road that had been cut in the side of the valley, mostly a few hundred feet above the river but sometimes practically at water level. Tourist accommodation in Srinagar is practically only houseboats, for "the beauty of the surrounds and tranquillity of the water". (*My answer to Brice's why? Later I learned how the British had these built, when laws forbade their owning lakeside residences back in the 1880s!*)

At Srinagar, much to my relief, Habib Thulla, the houseboat manager, came up with, "Major Pitt?"

"Yes," I replied.

"I am from the Soul Kiss."

We were off within half an hour. It was the closed season and like England: cool with the falling leaves and those that remain that enchanting rustic colour. On the seven mile drive, we passed many very English-looking houses.

I had been warned, by a rather disillusioned British architect in Calcutta, that the boats were all moored cheek by jowl with the owners loath to move them. This is indeed so. The Soul Kiss was moored on the bank of the Jhelum. Our taxi arrived at the opposite bank and a fifty-yard stretch of water separated us from the bow of the houseboat, which certainly looked as if she could do with a fresh coat of paint. We were relieved to find that we were the only occupants. Only one other boat, along the entire stretch, had been hired and that by a Bengali family. Although the boat could have been moved (by six men punting it down the river), it was not at all certain that we would then be re-connected to fresh water and electricity or so I was warned. We were very near the town and with so much river traffic, decided that it was far too interesting to

174

vacate. The boat, just over a hundred feet, had taken six months to build some five years earlier. There was a sitting-room with a stove, a dining-room on an uncomfortable sloping floor with no stove (so we hardly ever ate there.) There were two twin bedrooms, both en-suite. Above deck were tables and chairs for sunbathing, (had it not been so cold).

The food was actually prepared on a separate little shikara (skiff), a cooking boat. We also had the services of a very plush shikara to take us ashore and on all the river trips, at but 50p a day.

Though cold, the stoves had not been lit. The water was freezing. The lunch was disappointing (heated-up chicken) but there was a lovely bowl of fruit containing pears, apples and fat fresh walnuts, three times the size of any I had seen before. The décor was plain wood, with green curtains and covers to the three arm chairs, sofa and divan. There were plenty of little tables and a convenient desk at which I wrote this. In the evenings, the illumination varied between poor and nothing and more often than not, we had to resort to candles. A single one provided better illumination just as in Darjeeling.

After lunch we reclined on the "fully-sprung cushions", as proudly displayed on a notice above the gaily-coloured shikara, and were paddled down the river. One of our lasting memories are the friendly little bright blue and brown kingfishers which abound. These colourful birds with their long black beaks contrasted enchantingly with the austere November scene. They did not seem the least disturbed by our presence. They often hunt in pairs, diving repeatedly, though remarkably unsuccessfully, into the cold water. A pair perched on "Soul Kiss", completely ignoring us as we came and went.

Around much of the valley are hills and mountains and most of the arable land adjoins the river and lakes. The Kashmiri reclaim land to grow vegetables, on which their livelihood depends. First they ram stakes into the shallow portions of the lake, where the level is about four feet. They then drop stones to build a solid base; next they pour down earth and straw and gradually, month by month, add more compost. Once the mound has risen above the level of the water, green fronds that grow on the lake bottom, are dragged up and piled on top. Trees are planted round the sides to bind the soil and minimise loss during the floods of February and March. After a couple of years the reclaimed ground is highly fertile.

The water people also build floating islands which provide fertile feeding for birds in the way of frogs, lizards, mice, grasshoppers and insects. There we spotted a White Breasted Kingfisher (*Halycon smyrnensis*).

Most men take a daily bath. In January, when the lakes freeze over, they cut holes in the ice and continue this ritual.

It was most relaxing in the shikara, snug in our overcoats, scarves and hats, wrapped in thick blankets, with Rachel sleeping peacefully in her basket in the well of the boat. I read in the paper that morning that the temperature was 15°F warmer than normal! It was not long before the peace was disturbed by a shikara labelled "Grandfather & Son", which came alongside before rather inferior jewellery was passed over, none of which Anna liked. Next a boy, selling furs, glided over and Anna negotiated the cost of a fur hat and gloves for James. That night, much to our surprise, we had freshly cooked duck. The soup was delicious. We had our one and only hot bath of the week, and went to bed at 9 p.m. The fire stayed in till 11 pm. For the rest of the night we shivered.

We woke, frozen to the core and couldn't contemplate leaving our beds until Habib had lit the stove. By the time we reached the sitting-room for breakfast, a second had been lit and all was snug. The water, however, was so cold that when the plug stuck in the basin, it was too painful to pull out! Our breakfast was to be the best of the whole holiday: cornflakes and hot milk, beautifully cooked omelettes, toast, butter, marmalade and tea. By half past nine a huge crowd of hawker shikaras were waiting. First came the flower man, whose gondola was full of blooms. We bought chrysanthemums, purple asters, pink, red and white carnations, red, cream, yellow and white roses, marigolds and, most attractive of all, a huge bunch of dahlias. He asked a mere 75p: I paid him the 25p I had been advised! Next the photographic shikara arrived, but I had plenty of film. Then came the barber but it was far too cold even to contemplate a haircut; I needed all the insulation I could get. "Then just a massage?" he offered. Actually, a scalp massage, from an Indian hairdresser, is a very sensual experience. They drum the tips of their fingers on the scalp until it tingles. They even massage the eyebrows. Finally they run their hands smartly through the hair on each side of the head with such gusto that the hands clap together.

A boat, full of groceries, arrived but as we were not self catering, we needed nothing. However their persistence won, as we were accosted again on our way to Dal lake and yet a third time back at the boat. This time we bought a packet of Britannia biscuits and some chocolate (though both tasted distinctly stale). Another left a Kashmir stole with red borders, a green cape with lovely gold embroidery, and a Shah Touche scarf, made from the wool of the underbelly of young wild goats, found on the frozen lakes, amongst the high mountains in the Ladakh range and Shyok valley of Northern Kashmir, in January and February. The wool was extraordinarily soft and could easily be pulled through Anna's wedding ring. Habib told us that if you wrap an egg in a Shah Touche blanket, it will boil. They were incredibly warm but naturally very expensive. The goats are the Himalayan Ibex, also called Kail and Skya.

Another invited me to his factory and, four days later, I went there by <u>tonga</u>, a horse and carriage. I left Anna behind as it was a cold, wet, miserable day. Rain had fallen most of the night, the streets were covered in grey mud. On the way I watched the lock gates open and a whole flotilla of <u>shikaras</u>, loaded high with vegetables, rush forward into the river. I must have travelled through the foulest part of Srinagar on that <u>tonga</u> ride, bumping over pot-holes and squeezing past a lorry, whose back had fallen into the collapsed road. The journey had seemed unending until I finally arrived at the third bridge over the Jhelum. The people use the bridges to describe how to find their homes. Most are near the river, which plays an integral part in their lives and communications. Everyone knew exactly where you meant, when you mentioned the number of the particular bridge. I climbed some dirty steps to see men and boys working in disgusting conditions, making carpets, vastly inferior to the ones I had already seen. "No, I wasn't interested in carpets", I told him. So we took the <u>tonga</u> another hundred yards till we came to the shawl factory.

The hawkers became so persistent next day that Anna shouted: "Go away, you are ruining my holiday." They promptly left, saluting her, with: "Sorry to take your time." The trouble was that, outside the tourist season, they were desperate to sell their wares, and we had to suffer the full brunt of their brilliant though bullying salesmanship. We bought a tea cosy we didn't want from another who would just not leave until he had sold something – otherwise, he claimed, he would be unlucky. The same with the papier-mâché man. He showed me a vast collection of goods, beautifully made but none that I liked, except for the kingfishers, hand painted in gold leaf on platters. In the end I felt press-ganged into buying a paperweight. Finally the "skin boy" arrived and I bought a clouded leopard hat and a lynx hat for Anna. I enquired if he could get a leopard, tiger or bear skin. "Oh yes," he said, but first he and his villagers must make the kill. I was completely taken in by this, so I asked him to come back two days later with a skin. When he duly returned he told me he could get a tiger skin for 1,500 rupees, a bear skin for 600 rupees, a leopard for between for between 700 and 800, a clouded leopard, large, for 170 and small for seventy-five. I subsequently learnt at the furrier's and from Habib, that there were no tigers in the Kashmir forests and all the boy could have done was to make a deal with other traders. Habib's brother kills four to five Himalayan bears a season.

We had a delicious lunch of a duck stock soup, lamb chops which literally fell off the bone, and stewed pears. Soon after, we glided down the Jhelum to Dal lake where hardly a single houseboat, of the six hundred in Kashmir, was moored. The water was crystal clear. There was hardly a ripple. We clearly saw the green weed which is used to help reclaim the land. Dal lake is over ten feet deep. Punting was therefore impossible. The boat people use heart-shaped paddles and sit in the bow. We glided past the house where the Maharajah took tea each day and the long promontory, where the avenue was lined by poplars, down which he drove to be rowed over to the island. The trees were reflected in the water and the golden autumnal tint to their leaves was most picturesque against the silver bark.

We progressed into Dal lake. Right in the middle was the golden island, on which were three giant plane trees, called chenars. We first glimpsed the island, looking indeed golden, from miles away, with the afternoon sun.

There had been several terrorist incidents in Srinagar before the BBC crew arrived in 2003. I asked Michael Palin if he had ever been frightened. He thought not, just apprehensive, and volunteered that the peace and serenity of the lakes surpassed that of any other location of the whole "Himalaya" adventure.

From there we skimmed over to Nishat Bagh, which must be very beautiful in summer. The gardens were terraced and fountains normally play down the middle, when there is sufficient water from a river (dry in November). We waded ankle deep through leaves. By the time we had climbed to the top and back, we were extremely thirsty and for 10p our boatman had made a welcome pot of tea. On the homeward journey, we were blinded by the setting sun and had to let down the awning which thus obscured our view. As soon as the sun disappeared behind the mountains, it became bitterly cold.

That night we had duck stew, apple fritters and coffee, but that was the last as apparently it was expensive. I tried hard to keep the fire in all night and even managed to get the stove red hot at one stage. Once, while tending it, I put the top on the carpet. The result was a circular burn. I feared I would have to pay for a new carpet! Fortunately the mark mostly rubbed off and I needn't have worried as the bearer service was so bad that no one cleaned anything, let alone the carpet. At least we had a comfortable night with the heat lasting till 2 am.

It was a great relief to find no hawkers next day, but instead, Habib asked for dollars, so that his father could make the pilgrimage to Mecca. Foreign currency is extremely precious as it is not permitted to export a single Indian rupee. Anyway, I had none. Coincidentally Habib became even more mean over hot water. Anna's hands were almost frozen as she washed the baby's nappies.

HOUSE BOAT, SRINAGAR

CHAPTER 27

Carpets

A car took us to a carpet factory where a number of men and boys were busy at work. The carpets were so lovely that, thinking they were cheaper than they really were, we bought a rug similar to one in the Victoria and Albert Museum. Apparently when the Marquis of Bath visited Kashmir, he had been to the self-same factory and bought carpets for Longleat from the same man. He had paid no duty, but when ours arrived in England, months later, we were not so fortunate! We bought a rich red <u>bokara</u> and a small blue-and-grey rug, though these were only half completed at the time. We were invited to sign the back so we would know that they were the ones we had chosen.

All this time the owner had been puffing away on his hubble-bubble, looking for all the world a sheik. "The British have so much better taste than the Americans. We can sell the Americans anything". They did show us an astonishing Wild West carpet that they had copied from the napkin of a Texan millionaire. I subsequently learnt that Habib earns 3 per cent commission on these sales, so he made well over £6 on this deal alone. We photographed the men and boys outside, with the three carpets we had chosen and the tools they used, and were handed the history of each, while their designs were explained. Tea arrived while we were contemplating our purchases.

Later that evening, as I read the Indian newspapers, I learned of the devaluation of the pound sterling. My purchases had cost £40 more than I had estimated! Still, the rugs were very beautiful, and though they caused us a lot of anxiety over whether they would ever arrive and how much we might have to pay, once in our home in Reigate, we were very happy.

The flower <u>shikara</u> returned but with the season over, the blooms were already fading. However, we did buy a further 25p worth and Anna ordered bulbs, though few came up.

It was a bitter day and with a <u>kangri</u> (a small wicker basket, containing a pot of steaming charcoal and stone) and a blanket covering us, we set forth to explore the town, via the Jhelum, under the seven bridges. Anna held Rachel beneath her coat. As we were waiting at the lock gates for the water to rise, I pointed to how the lockkeeper was also keeping warm with a <u>kangri</u> under his coat. He noticed the gesture and indicated the bundle under Anna's coat. When I opened this to reveal Rachel, he laughed uproariously, joined by a group of women, fascinated by the blonde haired baby.

The river was used for everything: cleaning pots, clothes, washing carpets, cooking, dumping food and excretions. Others were blowing their noses into water that a few feet away a girl was drinking from. Carpets and clothes were cleaned by beating them on rocks by the bank of the river. We passed the carcase of a heifer, which was tied to the struts of a bridge in the middle of the water to keep fresh. Chickens were plucked while men were urinating into the water. I can only guess where they performed their bowel actions, and indeed where our own lavatory flushed into.

We glided under six of the seven bridges and despite a dull, overcast sky, caught glimpses of the snow-covered mountains. Our boatman had hired an extra hand, so we made good progress. We returned on a different stretch, where the river was practically blocked by floating logs, so barely able to squeeze through. We had lowered the canopy to pass under one particularly low bridge when a huge chunk of wood was hurled down on us. It missed the baby by a foot, landing heavily between Anna and me striking my camera case. This was to be the only hostile act we encountered – but very disturbing.

Opposite our houseboat was one of the most reputable shops in Srinagar called "Subhana the Worst". Though "very posh", there was little that appealed apart from green-blue material, with flowers down the middle, which would have made a lovely dress, but our funds had long since dried up. Subhana proudly handed us an old National Geographical Magazine with photographs of his shop.

On our last full day in Kashmir, we climbed the mountain which dominated the town. Habib showed us the route and was content to leave us, knowing he would not miss out as there were no shops! The weather had improved and this was our happiest day. It was a relief to be alone. The mountain, though little more than a thousand feet above the 5,500 feet of the valley, was a pretty stiff climb, but we were rewarded by a grand view of the whole area, noting the enormous amount of water. We appreciated how much of Dal and the smaller Nagin lake had been reclaimed. At the summit was one of Shiva's temples. We took off our shoes and climbed over the parapet. In the very middle was a large phallic symbol, like a giant black oxygen cylinder. A little Hindu priest-house was some fifty yards away.

In the afternoon we arrived at Nagin lake. Another shikara glided up to us and a long conversation took place between Habib and the boatman. Habib was buying triangular-shaped water chestnuts which grow well in the water some sixty miles from Srinagar. I had seen them for sale on the banks of the Jhelum not knowing what they might be. They tasted very like sweet chestnuts and considered a great delicacy. The boatman also had Cox's orange pippin. We bought a large tray for 10p, where a single apple had cost 5p in Delhi.

We celebrated our last dinner with goose, beautifully cooked and stuffed with whole almonds, which Habib carved in front of us. As we were leaving, we were presented with a bill for the wood. I couldn't believe we could be charged for this and enquired at the tourist office, to be told that this was indeed the custom. We returned to Delhi.

When the coach dropped us off at the airport office, the Imperial hotel was only a hundred yards away. It was very like the Oberoi. We were met by well dressed, polite staff and taken to a beautiful room. There was even hygienic paper over the lavatory seat. Our only criticism was, being near the kitchens, at the back, the service lifts were in action half the night.

At Kathmandu, we were met by Ralph and Ruth and taken to their home in a district called Rabi Bahun. Their residence, named the Round House, was actually two round houses joined together and once the home of the King's astronomer. They had made it very comfortable, even having added a sauna, probably the only one in Nepal.

Ralph pointed out the village of Kirtpur where the Newars had made their last stand in 1768, putting up a desperate resistance before every single one had had their nose and lips cut off. It was alleged that this amounted to one hundred kilograms.

That night we had a delicious meal of New Zealand lamb, followed by cherry tart. After dinner we enjoyed slides of Srinagar, which looked absolutely fabulous in the summer and I felt jealous that our visit had been so late in the year – yet so very different.

Kashmir has been called the "Switzerland of the Himalaya" and by the conquering Moghul emperors: "Paradise on Earth", with its beautiful mountain flowers, turquoise glacial lakes, pine forests and snowy mountains.

In the middle of the film-show, the lights failed – it was extraordinary how unlucky we were on this holiday – but Ralph had his own generator. Later two friends of Ruth arrived. They had just come back from Pokhara, where we were intending to visit next day. It had been raining continuously for seven days with the result there was nothing in the way of mountain scenery to see. They added that it was no place for a baby. Anna wisely elected to stay in Kathmandu.

CHAPTER 28

Pokhara

At Gaucher airport we met Tony, who was married to Jill, he reassured us that James was in fine fettle. The flight to Bhairawa was full of Chinese climbers. From there we drove to the Medical Reception Station (M.R.S.) at Paklihawa. My accommodation was a tent, erected on a brick base, with cupboards and mosquito netting. It was really very comfortable. I had the service of a splendid bearer who unpacked everything and brought steaming water so that I could have a wash. I next met Vishnu, the Nepalese doctor, who runs the M.R.S. and went round the wards, where I was consulted over some of the medical problems.

A new road was being cut through the mountains from Bhairawa to Pokhara, a distance of some hundred and twenty miles which would take three years to build. That afternoon we drove to view the new road, passing fields where groups of up to twenty villagers were harvesting each other's land. The crops were good and extended as far as the eye could see. It is a very fertile part of Nepal. We passed elephants, peacocks and the beautiful blue <u>healcant</u>, lophophourous, the national bird of Nepal which is called the danfe by the locals and has nine different coloured feathers. Across the road, strings had been tied from which wheat and rice were dangling. At Diwali, when the cow is worshipped, it is possible that the occasional animal may be missed, so if such an animal passes along the road, she will pass under these offerings, to be acceptable to the gods. It was all very much cleaner and more pleasant than Dharan. Driving along the newly-constructed road was extremely hazardous, worse even than our attempted journey along the Dhankuta road from Dharan. We slowly

188

passed hundreds of women breaking up rocks to be used as hard core for the road. Soon the dust was choking us and the conditions were no longer acceptable.

I was entertained most royally in the Mess that night until I excused myself while I could still stand. Next morning I flew to Pokhara, hoping to see Machapuchhare, the fishtail mountain, one of the most famous in Nepal, having a double peak. Sadly there was nothing to see. The same foul weather, that the friends of Ralph and Ruth had warned us of, was persisting. A friend advised me to fly straight back to Kathmandu, but all the flights were booked.

The tourist accommodation, just outside the airstrip, was better than I had anticipated, having sheets and blankets and even a wooden ceiling and walls in the corrugated hut. The food was dull, consisting mostly of rice and egg curry. Hurricane lamps provided the only illumination and after an early supper, I went to bed at 7 o'clock for a cold, uncomfortable night. I was up at 5 o'clock, half past five, 6 o'clock, and half past six, in attempts to see the peak, but each time it was invisible, until at last, at 11 o'clock, for just three minutes, the mountain appeared through a break in the clouds. The result was used for the cover of my first book.

Major Alistair Langlands was in Pokhara in his capacity as the senior officer in charge of Gurkha welfare and resettlement. He had been trekking in the mountains and had suffered early frost-bite. Having fixed him as best I could, he limped with me to the bazaar.

Again I tried to get out of town but the plane was full. Instead I explored the lakes, about three quarters of an hour's walk from the airport. On my way I disturbed a cobra, just two feet away. The first I was aware of was rustling in the leaves as the six-foot snake slithered away. A young boy rowed me over the lake, in a dug-out canoe, to a tiny temple, enchantingly set on a little island in the middle of the main lake.

Next morning Alistair and I watched a funeral procession pass below us, as we sat outside our accommodation. A white cloth, about six feet in length and eighteen inches wide, was carried, like a flag, by three men, on sticks, in front of the emaciated corpse, covered only by a saffron cloth. A group of twenty mourners followed. The body would either be burnt or thrown into the local river. Alistair warned how he studiously avoided washing in any sacred river, in case he came across a foot or something! He went on to explain that, after the funeral, the chief mourner would wear half the cloth as a turban, after shaving his head, and the remainder as a cummerbund for the thirteen days of grieving.

That afternoon I was lucky enough to secure the last seat on the plane. I was met by Ruth at Gaucher. She drove fast, though skilfully, through the streets like a racing driver. We visited, on the way, Annapurna Hotel, probably the best in Kathmandu. The following day, when ironically the weather was really beautiful, she took us back to the airport, passing a villager, balancing a baby with various pots on a yoke across his shoulders. We drove from Durbar Square to New Street, so named as the original had been destroyed by an earthquake thirty years before. On a blistering hot morning, we arrived forty minutes later at Dharan. An hour on, we were home. Doma had placed red roses, cut by Narbahadur, in the bedroom and the cases, with our Hong Kong purchases, had safely arrived from Calcutta, brought by rail with the Gurkha soldiers.

For about thirty seconds James, nearly twenty months, was too shy to join us. After that, he never left us. We were lucky, as we still had a few days of holiday left. On the very last day I was foolish enough to play football, during which I had my nose smashed by a kick from an embarrassed and apologetic

Gurkha soldier. I quickly set it before the pain came on. Next day I was hard at work.

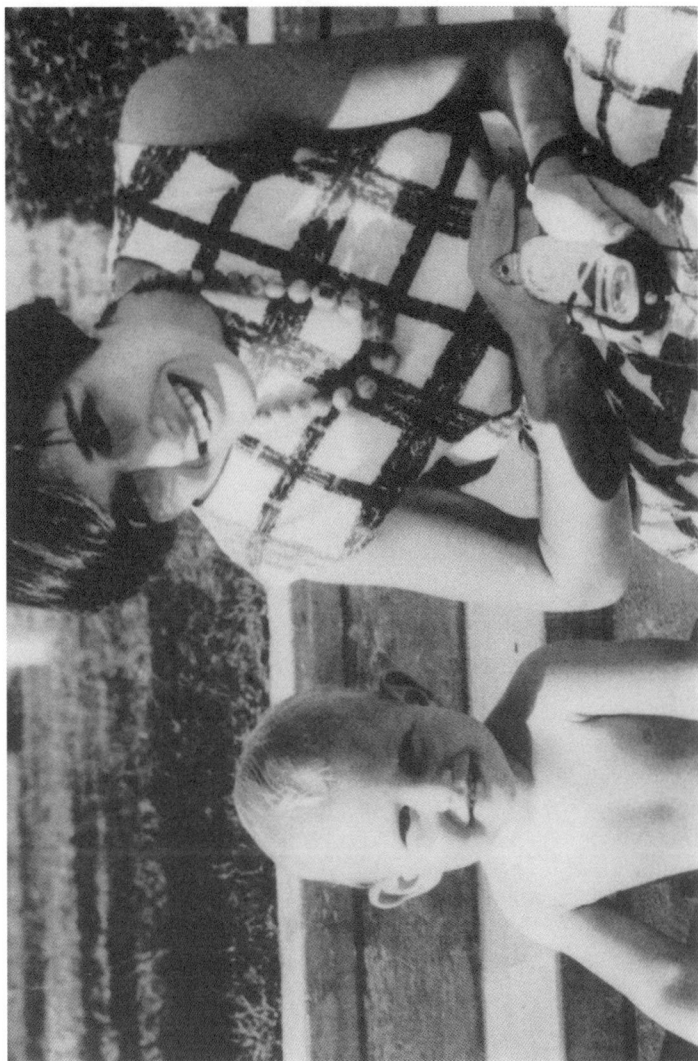

JAMES, ON HIS SECOND BIRTHDAY

FURTHER TROUBLES

Returning home after surgery.

CHAPTER 29

Acute Appendicitis

One of the rarest conditions in Nepal is acute appendicitis. However it still kills a number every year. Ramkumari was a twenty-year-old girl, who would have died but for the presence of the hospital. Nine days before I saw her, Ramkumari had developed the classical signs of acute appendicitis, the pain starting in the region just above the navel and settling in the right lower abdomen. She had been vomiting and ran a high fever. When she arrived, she was in a very poor state, with a rapid thready pulse and a huge mass in her tummy. Now nature deals with inflammation by trying to wall it off. This she does with the omentum, an apron of fat, which lies across the abdominal contents. This wraps itself around any diseased organ and that dreaded complication of generalised peritonitis is lessened. Ramkumari's appendix had blown up, burst and pus had poured out into the abdominal cavity but her omentum had dutifully sealed off the infection. However the bacteria were so virulent that the consequent abscess had enlarged to such a size that it must have contained two pints of pus. At any moment this could have burst into the rest of the peritoneal cavity and killed her. So we put Ramkumari to bed to minimise the risk of such a disaster and prescribed large doses of penicillin and streptomycin to kill the offending bacteria. Her guts had been paralysed by the sepsis and she was in a great deal of pain, due to the tension in the abscess. We gave her pethidine.

After forty-eight hours the crisis appeared to be over. Penicillin, which worked like a dream in Nepal, had cured yet another patient. Ramkumari's bowels started to function and she could pass flatus, a sure sign that the intestines are recovering. (We enquire about the passage of 'wind', after major abdominal surgery or when sepsis is present in the abdominal cavity. It is a relief to both patient and surgeon when it happens!) The mass diminished in size and over the next ten days, Ramkumari slowly improved until one day I noticed how her right knee was bent up. The abscess was enlarging again.

I changed the antibiotic to achromycin, which is useful in that it is effective against a wide range of bacteria and is taken by mouth. With this, her recovery continued and I was able to send her home, a month after her admission. (*I was later to learn that this drug will stain second teeth yellow, so should never be prescribed for children*).

Three months later, when her tummy felt quite normal, I readmitted Ramkumari and opened her up through a midline incision, to ensure that everything was all right, while at the same time removing the appendix. In this I made a double error. I had invited Ramkumari back too soon for what we term an 'interval appendicectomy' for, with such a huge abscess, the inflammation had not had time to settle completely. In addition, had I used the classical McBurney incision, right over the appendix, the operation would have been much easier. This is a much smaller cut and as virtually no muscle is divided, the discomfort is very much less. However, all went well. I removed a very stuck-down diseased appendix and she went home happily a week later.

Now why hadn't we operated straight away? In those days, I tried never to operate in the presence of an appendix abscess, as not only does the omentum seal off the infection but other organs, including the intestines, the womb, the ovary, the bladder and the front and back abdominal walls may help in walling it off. (*The pointing of the abscess on to the back wall of the abdomen, on the psoas muscle, had caused her knee to pull up, as that muscle had gone into spasm.)* In removing such a diseased appendix, any of these structures may first have to be freed. It is possible that they have become friable, due to the inflammation, and therefore easy to damage. In addition, during such a manoeuvre, pus could be spilt into the remainder of the abdominal cavity, so that the patient can end up with additional complications. *(These days (2005) this is no longer a problem as pus can be drained through a needle under ultrasound control, however we never had an ultrasound machine!)*

Though three months is usually long enough to allow inflammation to settle, if there has been surgical intervention or a very serious infection, as Ramkumari's, six months is a much safer period. By this time, nature has done such a wonderful job that there might not even be an adhesion present. (Adhesions are spidery strands that form after some operations.)

So why do we operate at all? The inside of the appendix remains diseased and a further attack of appendicitis may occur at any time; so we gamble that this will not happen during the three or six months wait. If it does, we operate at once, accepting that it might be a very difficult and hazardous operation.

*   *   *   *   *

So rare is appendicitis amongst the Gurkhas that, although I performed fifteen hundred operations in my first year, only six of these were appendicectomies, of which, the majority were 'cold', performed during a routine operating list.

When Captain Ratnabahadur presented with all the symptoms of an acute appendix, I assumed that he had developed a taste for Western food, while serving in the Far

East.   This would explain why he had the disease. Appendicitis is very rare in countries where a simple bland diet is norm.

It was a difficult appendicectomy, for Ratnabahadur had quietly nursed his appendix for four days until the pain had become too severe even for him. He made a good recovery, and was out of hospital in eight days. His wound had healed perfectly. He had no further fever.

I thought no more of him – not for five weeks. At that time Kali, a very pretty eight-year-old girl, came up with an exactly similar story. She too had had pain for four days. These Nepalese are so tough that they only seek help when desperate. She had all the signs and symptoms of acute appendicitis but, as an epidemic of typhoid fever was raging, I sent off a sample of her blood for the special typhoid investigation.

Now a very simple blood test, which is indicative of infection, can be readily performed, with a single drop of blood, obtained by finger prick. This is stained and examined under the microscope. The white cell count indicate a lot about disease. In health, the total white cell count per cubic millilitre of blood, varies from a low of about 3,000 to a high of perhaps 11,000.

There was no doubt about Kali's blood picture. She had a total white count of 20,000 of which 90% were polymorphs, the type of white cell which multiplies when infection is present. The property of these cells is to engulf bacteria, by an amoeboid process, to destroy them.   Kali's blood picture suggested a serious infection, quite unlike the picture in typhoid fever, where the total white count is often very low.

Again it proved a very difficult appendix to remove; yet again the patient made a good recovery. Two days later the test for typhoid came back. It was positive, she had typhoid fever with acute appendicitis as a complication. A few days later I repeated the test, which we call the Widal. It had now risen to well over 1/640; this supported our assumption that Kali not only had typhoid but the attack had been quite serious, yet she had no other symptom.

$$* \qquad * \qquad * \qquad * \qquad *$$

Four days later Bhimprasad, a pensioner's son, and a seventeen-year-old student at the cantonment Gurkha school, came with abdominal pain; he also had suffered severe pain for four days. His total white count was also 20,000 and he too had all the symptoms an acute appendicitis. In addition, in the past three days, he had found that he could hardly walk, indicating that his swollen appendix also lay against the psoas muscle. Even in the presence of this sepsis, he had tried to play basket-ball, though had soon to give it up!

Bhimprasad had been nursing a perforated gangrenous appendix. I had to drain half a pint of pus before I could remove the grossly diseased organ. He made an excellent recovery, but I thought that it would be wise to test his blood. Typhoid it turned out to be!

$$* \qquad * \qquad * \qquad * \qquad *$$

This was truly extraordinary. We then gave thought to the Gurkha captain. Even though five weeks had elapsed, and he had no pain, fever or any other complaint, we sent off his blood. To our astonishment this too turned out to be typhoid fever. Thus a soldier, who had been subjected to the unpleasantness of several T.A.B injections in his career, could still develop typhoid. (T.A.B stands for the anti-typhoid inoculation. The "T" part is typhoid while the "A" and "B" stand for Paratyphoid A and B. Though the latter diseases are less serious, they can still kill from such complications as internal haemorrhage and perforation.) We now checked Ramkumari's blood – taken when she had been so ill. Her Widal had also been positive. This was by no means the end of acute appendicitis, for the typhoid epidemic was to run till the end of the rainy season.

CHAPTER 30

Stillbirth - an Obstetric Disaster

Narvadadevi was only fifteen, yet looked nearer thirty when we admitted her. She was lucky in that her life was easy to save, but how she suffered in those days before she arrived!

Her husband, Bhupalsing, though only nineteen, was already a very wealthy man by Nepalese standards. It was this that saved Narvadadevi's life. He owned thirty buffloes, twenty cows, and enough land to be able to sell rice. They lived in a village called Madhu Malla, some thirty-eight miles away.

Narvadadevi had gone into labour five days before her arrival. The second day her waters burst and then that awful complication of obstetrics occurred: obstructed labour.

The problem was simple enough, Narvadadevi was too small for the delivery of a full-term baby, her pelvis was just not wide enough. She had pushed and strained but the baby would not come. The neighbours came to help and they pressed and pummelled but all to no avail. The ominous signs of foetal distress occurred, as the unborn baby became more and more upset by the pushing and shoving. The baby started having his bowels open and the stools coloured the leaking waters green. This is meconium staining. The inevitable happened, Narvadadevi no longer felt him kicking, the baby had died.

A serious complication now set in. The head of the little boy was so firmly stuck that it obstructed her bladder. She could no longer pass urine. This frightful condition lasted four whole days. This was an incredibly dangerous situation, as the kidneys could easily have stopped functioning, this would inevitably have killed her within a week or two. It must have been agonisingly painful.

At last Bhupalsing decided he must get help and fifteen villagers made the journey to Dharan, starting at 3.00 am. They carried her, slung in a <u>doli</u> (hammock), two at a time, eleven men carrying her in turn. They were all either friends or employees of Bhupalsing, so he did not have to pay porterage fees, only the cost of food on the journey, about fifty rupees in all.

The continuous jolting, which inevitably occurred with every step, assisted the progress of the baby and by 7.00 am the baby's head was born, though still she couldn't pass urine or rid herself of the dead baby.

When they finally arrived that same afternoon, the poor girl was exhausted. Her father-in-law had gone ahead, to warn us they were on their way. We sent him back by ambulance, shortening the journey a little. What a relief the sight of the vehicle must have been! A four-day-old still-born baby is not a pretty sight, nor do the flies and smell help. We took her straight to the labour ward and tried to pass a catheter to relieve the obstructed bladder. She was however so swollen that it was very difficult to find the correct opening. Even when we succeeded, no urine flowed. The baby's shoulders were now the cause of the obstruction. We took hold of the macerated head and rotated it into the correct position for the subsequent delivery. It was however a very large baby and his shoulders were stuck solid in the pelvis. As the stillborn baby was at last delivered, the bladder emptied with such a gush that it was impossible to collect all the urine; what we caught measured four pints and what soaked me must have been at least a pint! The little dead boy weighed 7 lbs 12 oz, a heavy weight for our hospital, where most weighed around 6 lbs.

With the delivery of the baby, most of Navadadevi's worries were over. We prescribed heavy doses of antibiotics to prevent infection, otherwise this might have been her one and only baby, as sterility could result. We stopped her breasts producing milk, by binding them tight, and giving stilboestrol. We observed her very carefully to see if she would produce urine. Her bladder had been so stretched that the muscle had 'at first' lost its power to contract. We left in a self-retaining catheter, releasing it every three to four hours. The tone in the bladder returned remarkably quickly, one big advantage of being so young.

Two days later she could pass her water naturally and five days after the long journey to Dharan, we let her go, her only complication being occasional incontinence, for the nerves of her bladder had also been stretched and these would take longer to recover. In a month or so she would have no further problems, though, I fervently prayed, they wouldn't try for another too soon!

CHAPTER 31

And when the Bough Breaks......

Guarding the hungry <u>bakra</u> (goats).

Finding sufficient food for the goats is a considerable problem in the dry season, for the grass has either withered or long since been cropped by these demanding animals. Young men and boys may have to reach high into trees to cut down branches of leaves, as fodder. Being almost as agile as monkeys, especially using their bare toes, these disturbing heights hardly seem to bother them. However, though they might climb like monkeys, they do not fall like them and many ghastly accidents occur.

One afternoon, Anna and I were walking along the new road being constructed from Dharan to Dhankuta. This zig-zag route through the mountains was being built with "free" labour: every village had to detail a certain number to work on the road for a specified time. The British loaned a bulldozer which saved many hours of back-breaking work. However, as no culverts were constructed, nor steep banks supported, we dreaded the damage the monsoon must do, once it broke. Subsequently we learnt that this was of course expected and it was where the road was blocked, that culverts and supports would be placed, during the following dry season. To my sceptical mind, that would mean placing culverts every few feet along the entire road. During our walk, we watched langur monkeys with their four-foot tails leaping from tree to tree and crashing into the foliage below. As we made for home, we were passed by an army three ton lorry. The driver offered us a lift, saving an hour's walk. We stopped at the surgical ward where I enquired of the Sister if all was well. She was most relieved to see me because Bharat, a fourteen-year-old, had just been admitted.

How fortunate it was that the truck had brought us back early. Bharat had climbed a tree, similar to the one we had watched the monkeys playing in. As he slipped, his weight snapped a branch, the broken end of which had ripped open his belly. His intestines were hanging out.

All this had happened six hours ago at Barachattra, by the side of the Kosi, fourteen miles away, - in fact in the same direction the truck had just come.

Fortunately the hole in Bharat's tummy was so large that the blood vessels, feeding the protruding guts, were not constricted and the bowel remained viable. The Sister had immediately covered it all with a hot sterile pack and it was, at this stage, that I appeared. We took him straight to theatre and replaced the intestines. I next removed a large portion of dirty fat, the omentum, which had come out with the intestines. I trimmed the ragged, bruised edges of the gash so it could heal soundly. I removed all the bits of bark lying in and around the wound and even on the surface of the bowel. Finally I enlarged the wound considerably to examine the rest of the contents, to ensure that I had missed nothing, neither dirt nor damage. After I had closed the wound, he was left with an inverted "T" so that, when he looked down, he would always see a "T", T for tree. I made sure that he learnt that much English! Next day his condition was causing us concern. This I could not readily understand, for he had had a relatively simple operation and appeared a strong lad. I was resting his damaged bowel, by feeding with an intravenous drip, at the same time keeping his stomach empty, with the help of a Ryle's tube, which I had passed through his nose into his stomach. We were sucking up a great deal of stale blood. Although this could have been due to the tube, as it may occasionally bruise or abrade the gullet while being passed, more likely it was bruising of his stomach and intestines in the fall.

It was however his chest that was my main concern. Before the operation this had sounded perfectly clear, now his breathing was so laboured that he hadn't even the strength to cough. A chest x-ray showed that his heart had moved from its normal place in the left chest over to the right, that his windpipe had moved from the mid-line also to the right, and the right diaphragm was markedly raised. There was, in addition, a triangular shadow at the base of his right lung. All this implied an almost complete collapse of the whole of the right lung, especially the lower lobe. The latter is a recognised complication of any operation to the upper abdomen, but very rare indeed in a young fit boy. Something was obstructing his airway.

I turned him on his side and repeatedly chopped away at his chest with the edge of my hands, forcing him to cough. (We never had the luxury of a physiotherapist). At last, after two exhausting hours of pummelling, to which he protested feebly, he coughed up a large stone. Immediately his breathing eased as his lung re-expanded.

He had been chewing a lychee, while cutting branches with his kukri; he must have finished the fruit and been sucking the stone at the time of his accident. The shock of the fall had caused him to inhale deeply and the stone had entered his right main bronchus, the air passage to his right lung. The stone is nearly an inch long and a quarter of an inch wide. It could easily have lain across the corina, where the main airway, the trachea, divides into the bronchi to feed each lung. He would then have died of asphyxia in a few moments. Before the operation, the stone had lain loosely in the bronchus so that air by-passed it. It was the pressure of the anaesthetic gases that had made it stick firmly resulting in the collapsed lung.

A second x-ray showed that the heart had returned to its normal position, yet the lower lobe, about a third of the lung, was still collapsed. It was now two and a half days and I had not yet allowed him anything by mouth, as there are two common complications to such an accident. The first is infection, as peritonitis may occur, unless all the dirt is scrupulously removed and antibiotics given to kill bacteria which must have entered with the branch. We had given the boy injections of penicillin, streptomycin and anti-tetanus serum immediately on arrival. The shock to the intestines of being exposed to the outside world, may cause the second complication: the guts to be temporarily paralysed, a condition termed paralytic ileus. The intestines fill up with fluid and peristalsis, the method used to propel food along the lumen, ceases. The condition is exacerbated by food and fluids, as these add to the distension of the bowel. This explains why we "drip and suck" after abdominal surgery, to lessen the chance of ileus. We keep the intestines as empty as possible, by aspirating the gastric fluids through the Ryle's tube ("suck") and by feeding the patient through a vein ("drip").

Back in England, the loss of body heat from exposed bowel would be a substantial, especially after all these hours, but in the tropics, where the temperature on this particular Sunday afternoon, at the end of February, approached that of the human body, no significant loss occurred, apart from fluid through invisible perspiration.

I listened to his abdomen with my stethoscope. It was silent. It had not yet started functioning. Yet it was the collapsed portion of lung that remained my main concern. We kept thumping away at Bharat's chest, attempting to dislodge whatever was still blocking the air tube. In addition we raised the bottom of his bed, hoping that the obstruction might clear by gravity; but the lobe remained collapsed!

Next day, as I listened, I could hear bowel sounds. Normal peristalsis was returning. I looked at the in take and output chart by his bed. I noticed that very little fluid was being aspirated. I asked if he had passed any wind "down below". He told us that he had, during the night. These are the cardinal signs that the guts were returning to normal. I could safely dispense with the Ryle's tube, which anyway tends to make people chesty; I took down the drip. Now that we could start walking him around, I thought the obstruction must surely clear. But no! At first we allowed him only two ounces of milk and water hourly. Soon we were able to give him as much fluid as he wished. Finally, when I knew his insides had fully recovered, I explained: "Put your hands firmly on each side of your tummy, this will help support the wound and cause you less pain. Now if you cough loudly ten times you can have some food," for he was very hungry!

"Ek, dui, teen, char, panch, cha, sath, ath, nau, das," I counted slowly as he coughed each time, though the last few efforts were pretty feeble! "Now if you do that every hour, you can have as much food as you like," I promised.

It worked! Next day his chest had fully expanded. I never did find out what had caused the residual collapse. It had probably been a plug of thick mucus that had formed when the stone was present.

*　　*　　*　　*　　*

Huge loads of fire wood for the market.

When Tekbahadur arrived at the B.M.H. one evening, early in October, having fallen from a tree, I found it rather surprising. By the beginning of October, the last of the rains are falling and the grass is still green. It is not until well into that month that the men and boys must climb trees for fodder.

Tekbahadur had fallen twenty feet off a sal (sakkhuwa) tree. He had trodden on a dead branch and had fallen head first, landing on his forehead, breaking his fall and thus saving his life, with his arms, at the cost of fracturing both wrists and shoulder, as well as sustaining a very severely bruised chest. I manipulated his bones into their correct position.

"Were you cutting food for goats?" I later asked. "No," came the unexpected reply, he was plucking the large leaves to sell in the market. He explained how he tacked these together with something akin to pine needles, to form a temporary disposable plate to last a meal. These plates are called duna. It took five hours of hazardous climbing to pick sufficient to earn two rupees in the market. The large leaves are high in the tree, the lower ones having long since been plucked.

I remembered seeing villagers coming out of the forest with two or three bundles of similar leaves, which they had tied together with grass, as we might a bundle of papers with string. I had wondered why they were carrying so little, while their colleagues, more often the women, were weighed down with great loads of firewood. I hadn't realised, until this conversation, just how much hard work had gone into the collection of these small bundles.

The sakkhuwa provides the most valuable timber in Nepal. All the local furniture and fittings are made from this. It is very durable, though expensive. The sleepers of the little railway line which brought many of our patients from Chattra were made from this wood.

Tekbahadur didn't have to stay long and a month later, when I saw him in Out-Patients, his bones had knit soundly in a perfect position.

*　　*　　*　　*　　*

One use of sal wood (sleepers).

Fifty-eight-year-old Ramnath had too large a family to support from a small plot in the hills, so he was forced to move, leaving behind his wife and eldest son, while he came down into the terai with the rest of his family.

Ramnath had had eleven children. Three of his sons had died, while three others had settled in Ceylon (Srilanka). He made the move with his remaining children, two daughters and two sons. He bought land and started building his new home when disaster struck when only half completed. Seven hours before his admission, he was eighteen feet up a tree, hacking a large bough for his house with his kukri. The branch he was actually standing on gave way. That was as far as the house would get during the rest of that and the whole of the following year.

As I examined him, after his long journey, I felt crackles of air over the whole of the left side of his chest and abdomen; he had ruptured his lung and the escaping air had entered the tissues, a condition called surgical emphysema. His pelvis was acutely tender, for here his bones had sprung apart like an opened oyster shell. His right femur had been driven so hard into its socket, the acetabulum, that the latter had shattered, a condition termed "central dislocation of the hip".

He had passed no urine since his fall. I inserted a catheter; blood-stained urine came out. In addition he was acutely tender over his left loin, where I could palpate a doughy mass. He had signs of a damaged left kidney. This I subsequently confirmed by an intravenous pyelogram.

His abdomen was severely bruised and because of this, he tightened his abdominal muscles as I examined him; this we term 'voluntary guarding'. He could easily have internal injuries, as well as the damaged kidney, so I allowed him nothing by mouth, feeding him with intravenous fluids until he passed flatus, some forty-eight hours later. Slowly everything improved, his kidney recovered, the burst lung sealed itself, expanded and the escaped air absorbed.

After ten days I let him home on crutches, having first offered to extract his loose and decayed teeth but he told me he would rather keep them. The Nepalese are loathe to lose any part of their bodies!

I saw him again but not until nearly a year later when he walked confidently into my consulting room. He told me first how his seventeen-year-old son had made the home practically waterproof, by laying a straw roof and the five were living happily in the completed half of the house. Ramnath had only come as he had contracted dysentery and wanted that treated, otherwise he had made a full recovery and was planning to start again on the house before the next monsoon.

GOING HOME

A mother holding the hoe end   that had been tied to the cord, when the afterbirth had been retained.

CHAPTER 32

"My ghastly mistake"

One of my most terrible mistakes was over Kharkabahadur, a strong nineteen-year-old, who had fallen forty feet out of a tree, while cutting down branches to make climbing frames for beans, cucumbers and climbing spinach that grew so well.

Kharkabahadur was an orphan; he had neither married nor had relatives. He was employed by a man who owned land. He arrived twenty-four hours after the accident, by which time he had a huge swelling over his lower back, a cut on his head and was coughing up blood. He had obviously broken his spine but, to my surprise, he could still move his feet; he was not paralysed.

Very carefully, I x-rayed him and discovered that, not only had he a severe fracture-dislocation of his lumbar spine, his lower backbone, but also he had punctured his right lung. He had a pneumothorax, air filling the space in his chest which is normally occupied by the expanded lung.

I should have operated immediately, but I didn't. I should have decompressed the spine and bolted or wired the bones together, so that they could not move. The spinal cord runs right through these vertebrae and if these bones rotate too much, the cord can be sheared, resulting in immediate and lasting paralysis.

The operating theatre had been closed for re-decoration and it meant operating, without air-conditioning, in a side-ward, with the temperature 94°F (about 36°C), doing a particularly difficult and hazardous operation. I was also very tired, having just completed a long and exhausting out-patients session in that heat.

I gave the ward staff detailed instructions about Kharkabahadur's condition and in particular how they must turn him. This they were to do gently, with a very minimum of two orderlies, so that no twisting of his broken spine must occur.

The staff tried very hard but none are trained in skilled nursing and of course, as I should have realised, disaster struck. He was turned by one orderly on his own; the well meaning nurse simply tugged Kharkabahadur's shoulders over. The lad's pelvis stayed where it was. When I did my ward round that same night, I found Kharkabahadur to be paralysed, less that twenty-four hours after he had been admitted. How I cursed myself for the inexcusable delay in operating.

A paralysed man in Nepal, what was his future? There remained just a glimmer of hope as he could still move the toes of his left foot, was conscious of passing urine and had some sensation in his skin which at least would prevent him developing bed sores. I wired his spine together that same night, having first inserted a tube into his chest to allow the trapped air to escape.

What a remarkably brave and contented patient Kharkabahadur was at first. Every time I entered the ward, he smiled gratefully, politely saluting me with namaste. He never grumbled. His punctured lung healed quickly and the escaped air absorbed. I had made him a plaster jacket. It was the monsoon, when the humidity is very high, approaching 100 per cent. The plaster took a long time to dry and needed much re-enforcing before strong enough to support his broken spine.

The monsoon is also a difficult time for drying laundry; we had to erect clothes-lines under the covered verandah and, as soon as the rain stopped, put the washing out in the sun before the next torrential storm. Even then the clothes took a long time to dry. Another complication of the humidity is mould.

This grows rapidly and thickly on most articles, especially leather and films. Practically any material can be ruined in a few days and during our first monsoon, we used to hang suits and clothes out in the sun, whenever it was dry, keep cameras in air-tight containers with drying powder, to prevent mould growing on the lenses, and wipe leather goods, including books, every day. This was such a performance that we fitted electric light bulbs in the cupboards and a sixty-watt bulb provided sufficient heat to dry the air, thus slowing the growth of mould. We also had our air conditioner and this, by lowering the humidity as well as the temperature, helped preserve our belongings.

I made use of both these methods to dry out Kharkabahadur's plaster, using a cradle of electric light bulbs with an aluminium cover, which at least dried the surface. I next put Kharkabahadur, in his plaster, in an air-conditioned side ward for a couple of days, to dry it further.

Finally, with his wound well healed, the time came to go home, as by now he had learnt to manage his bladder and bowels and we were doing little more than feeding him. Porters and a buffalo cart were arranged and he was taken back to his master's house.

"Return in three months and we will remove your plaster," I promised; by then his bones should have knitted, though I knew his spinal cord would never recover.

Several weeks later, I found Kharkabahadur lying on a stretcher in reception. It was certainly nowhere near the time I had asked him to return, although just sufficient for the bones to have knitted. I removed his plaster, x-rayed his spine and found the wires in perfect position. He had obviously been looked after very well. He was well nourished and there were no bed-sores.

I gave him vitamins and told him to return. There was little else I could do. Then the story came out, his employer would no longer look after him; he had arranged for Kharkabahadur to be carried back to hospital and "dumped"! The porters had vanished.

A paralysed orphan in Nepal, not a relative to help him. There was not even a surgical bed available; there was nowhere for the lad to go.

I hardened my heart. "You'll have to go", I told him. It was however still the monsoon season; a landrover wouldn't be able to manage the tracks, it meant porters and a buffalo cart but the men were busy in the fields. It would take time. I borrowed one of my colleague's medical beds until able to discharge a patient.

As it worked out, it had been advantageous to admit Kharkabahadur and the bed was not wasted. His neglected joints were terribly stiff and these had to be exercised. It was a week before he could even sit in a chair. Every day we moved his joints that little bit more and he learned tricks with tapes which were tied to his big toes in order to pull his feet up.

Then one day Brigadier Taggart, on one of his periodic strolls round the hospital, heard the pathetic tale and felt so sorry for Kharkabahadur, that he promised to try to find him a job in the cantonment, perhaps as a tailor.

With such incentive, we bought a couple of bicycle wheels and managed to procure a chair from the quartermaster. We persuaded the engineers to construct a wheelchair with these. It took time but eventually it arrived and Kharkabahadur was able to push himself around, which he did at great speed.

Kharkabahadur was, without doubt, a very bright lad. Matron gave him painting and needlework to pass the time. Finally he was given accommodation in the soldiers' lines, with a free bed, food and a constant supply of clean water.

By this time, he had even learnt to stand on his own. But in these months he had become despondent. He had been provided with *bidis* whilst in the ward and now he sent messages up to the hospital demanding more. At first Ranjit paid for these out of his own pocket. He soon had to stop this generous action.

Kharkabahadur became more morose once the supply of cigarettes dried up, but I expect he managed to "cadge" some from the soldiers! He was offered further instruction in needlework but had lost interest. When I left, he was still in the soldiers' lines, completely idle. He had his mobile wheelchair but no work. He simply didn't want to do anything.

I went to visit him on my very last day in Nepal, with a box of *bidis*, which I had asked Narbahadur to procure in the bazaar.

He stood to thank me with namaste! Had he learned a method of rising or could there have been actual recovery? My transport to the airport was due in a few minutes, I had no time to assess him. Could this be a miracle? I will never know.

CHAPTER 33

Leaving the Hospital

Hemlata bearing her gifts.

We left Dharan two years after our arrival, physically exhausted. I had worked flat out since our return from Kashmir being "on call" twenty four hours a day, without a single break. One day, after spending practically the whole day in the theatre, I had to perform a worrying operation on a Gurkha soldier, who had just arrived by helicopter from Paklihawa. He had not passed urine for three days. I explored one of his kidneys to insert a tube, so that urine could escape while the kidneys, blocked by stones, might recover. Next day I felt terribly ill myself. But still emergencies rolled in. I remember having to remove the afterbirth, following delivery of a baby, and to extract a large branch that had jammed between the two forearm bones of an old man who had fallen out of a tree, while running a high fever myself. Fortunately there were no more real emergencies and I was able to stay in bed a couple of days. However, on the third, a little boy, suffering from a stone in the bladder, couldn't bear the pain any more. Children develop these from deprivation. Almost certainly they do not drink enough, are malnourished and possibly the mineral content of the water is unusually high. It was an easy diagnosis, for the little boys come pulling their penises from the awful pain caused by these stones. Sometimes, they have suffered so long, and have tugged their little "willies" so much, that the organ had actually lengthened considerably. We confirmed the diagnosis by a simple x-ray, and the removal of the stone is a relatively simple operation. That morning I also had to amputate the arm of a little girl who had been crushed by a tree. I was glad when the day was over.

*   *   *   *   *

It is the custom at the British Military Hospital to present departing Doctors and Nursing Sisters with a gift. I was presented with a silver kukri (used to illustrate the spine of my first book), silver cuff links, in the form of crossed kukris, and silver tiepin in the shape of a kukri.

Damaraj, once a cowherd, now responsible for patients' documentation, delivered a farewell speech, in which he recounted how the patients referred to me as the "Bosnos Doctor". (Whenever they came in to my consulting-room I said "bosnos", which implies, "Do sit down").

Helmlata, my interpreter, gave us a little brass drinking vase, with matching bowl for rice and two plates. Anna used to send her parcels from England for many years.

We left our bungalow at 8 am that last day. The drive from our home was lined by nurses, each with at least one garland of flowers joined together like a daisy-chain. In turn the staff stepped up to hang these around our necks. Only James escaped; he couldn't bear anything encircling him. The fragrance was gorgeous. I was almost suffocated by the amount. Others placed a chain of gauze, in lieu of flowers, apparently a Buddhist custom. They all saluted us with namaste as we finally drove past. We couldn't have had a kinder send-off anywhere in the world. Further down the road we were stopped for huge bunches of jacaranda and garlands of frangipani. Once out of sight, we quickly shook them off, because of the insects!!

Garlanded.

It was a blustery day, the flags taut with barely a ripple. The plane was delayed, so we sent Doma, Sorat, and Kanchi home. James, two years and three months old, clung desperately to Doma's neck. It almost broke my heart prising his desperate fingers from her neck. Minutes later he was playing happily in the landrover with: "Doma's gone." Rachel slept.

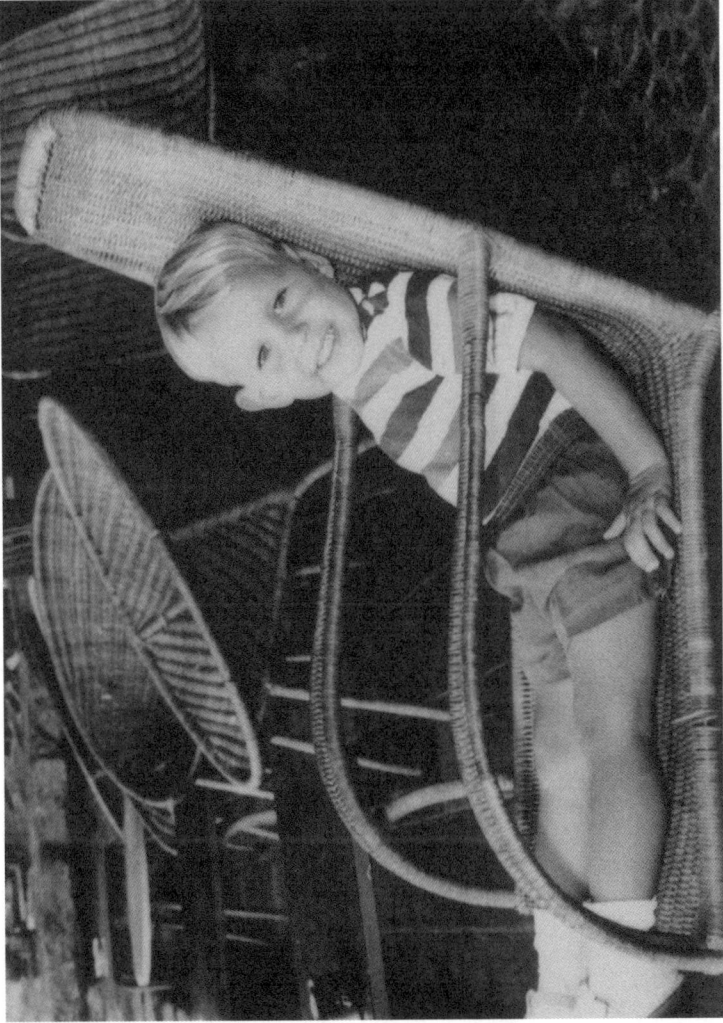

HOMEWARD BOUND

EPILOGUE

Treating a fractured femur by "gallows".

Epilogue

There can be no better way of recording the drama in the last few days of the hospital than by the following story.

The Daily Telegraph, Monday, August 29 1988

Tales of true grit as a Raj outpost goes out in glory

The British Army base at Dharan, Nepal, was caught in the middle of the earthquake that rocked the Himalayan kingdom and northern India last week. Now it finds itself at the epicentre of relief efforts. JAMES BONE reports:

WHENEVER the monsoon rain relents and light breaks through the heavy cloud, a helicopter swoops down on Dharan Cantonment, bringing more casualties from the Himalayan foothills. It lands amid admiring locals in a field on the edge of the camp.

A team of camouflage-clad British combat medics immediately sprints towards it and, gingerly, unloads the matchstick-limbed peasants on to stretchers.

Operation Nightingale, the Army's effort to help those injured in last week's earthquake, is in full swing.

The Army base at Dharan, the Gurkha headquarters in Nepal, has become the hub for attempts to rescue victims still trapped in their villages, often many days walk into the hills.

The camp, which houses a British military hospital, lies just 30 miles from the epicentre of the quake.

By the weekend, the 75-bed hospital had treated about 700 Nepalis, and had admitted 183. But casualties were still coming in from remote villages lost in the verdant foothills of Everest. By the end of this week, the hospital expects to have more than 250 patients.

Staff at the camp, who yawn and totter now from fatigue, tell a tale of true British grit. As Lt-Col Michael Kefford, the camp commander, put it: "We started 30-love down and the team has played an absolute blinder. It is Brits at their best."

The weekend of Aug 21 began in a typically rum fashion for this little slice of England on the doorstep of the Himalayas, the last British Army cantonment in the Indian sub-continent.

On Friday night, a rogue elephant in search of bananas broke down the main gate and rampaged through the camp. The brute tried to tear the roof off a bungalow belonging to one of the grooms. But he was seen off.

Saturday was rather more jolly. The base, which has about 70 British personnel, was full of children over from the "UK" for the school holidays.

Under the first scorching sunshine for weeks, their parents dutifully organised an "It's a Knockout" tournament.

The Seven Brides of Dracula, led by Lt-Col Kefford, came out on top. Elated, the competitors – now lightly fried by the sun – feasted at a barbecue.

The children were put to bed, under the watchful eyes of their Nepali ayahs (nannies), and the merrymaking went on into the night. It was the stuff Indian summers are made of.

232

At 4.54 and 43 seconds on Sunday morning, all that changed. Major Ronald Bailie and his wife, Ruth, from Northern Ireland, thought the elephant had returned.

Major Neil Ineson dived under his bed. Capt Susan Pratt clung to hers in case the ground opened up.

Mrs Camilla Sanders, who slept through it all, awoke several hours later to find all her possessions strewn on the floor and exclaimed that she had been burgled.

A 40-second earthquake, measuring 6-7 on the Richter scale, had rumbled through eastern Nepal and northern India. It was the worst quake to hit Nepal since Black Monday, in January 1934, when 8,500 died.

Within minutes, Lt-Col Peter Guy, the Dharan base's senior medical officer, telephoned Lt-Col Kefford, suggesting that the hospital should put into effect its emergency contingency plan.

Lt-Col Kefford sent a staff sergeant out to check damage to the camp. He returned to report that the rows of bungalows built to be earthquake-proof 30 years ago had suffered only superficial damage.

The only casualties within the base were the son of a hospital worker, whose arm had been badly cut by falling glass, two Gurkha soldiers and two locally employed civilians.

But the story in Dharan itself was altogether different. By 5.30am casualties had already begun arriving at the camp's main gate.

Lt-Col Kefford told the hospital to adopt its "crash" procedure. An hour later, a casualty clearing centre was already functioning in several rapidly erected tents at the gates.Half a dozen army wives, who had medical training, were assessing which of the wounded needed hospital treatment.

"There was just a sea of Nepali faces, and it began to rain turning the entire scene into a quagmire," said Mrs Gillian Leatherday, who served as an army nurse before marrying her staff-sergeant husband.

"Like British wives always do – we coped".

By mid-afternoon, staff at the camp had seen 450 casualties, three of whom had died. About 150 had been admitted to the hospital. That day, Lt-Col Guy performed 27 operations.

Dharan town was in ruins, with 135 dead, and the hospital braced for more casualties to flood in from the outlying villages. Three British army medical teams flew from Hong Kong, and two RAF Hercules arrived at nearby Biratnagar Airport with 18.5 tons of tents, generators, blood and medicine.

The military hospital began to take patients from the rudimentary hospitals at Dharan and Biratnagar. In mid-week, Nepalese army helicopters began ferrying injured to the camp from the hills.

The pilots reported that many inaccessible villages had collapsed or been swamped by landslides. The official death toll in Nepal was around 700 at the weekend, and rising.

"We understand there are still hundreds of casualties to come out of the hills," said Lt-Col Kefford. " I expect to get 70 a day for as long as it takes." Casualty figures may run into thousands.

In a way, it was lucky that the earthquake happened when it did. Within the next two years, Britain plans to vacate Dharan and turn it over to the Nepalese government, continuing Gurkha recruitment and administration from Kathmandu.

The existence of the British base at Dharan has long been an embarrassment to the Nepalese government, a member of the Non-Aligned Movement and a leading proponent of a South Asian "zone of peace".

It is not clear what will happen to the base. Even if, as seems likely, the hospital continues to function, the last cantonment of the Raj – an oasis of neatly trimmed lawns and whitewashed bungalows – is sure to die.

But, with its vital role in earthquake relief, it is going out in a blaze of glory.

James visited the hospital twenty years after we had left. There he met Ranjit Rai, now superintendent of the hospital and told him his father used to work here.

Who? Peter Pitt.

Major Pitt? You must be James!!

Last time I saw you, you were this high, pointing to his waist!

James was taken to the theatre library and was shown photographs of Narmaya, whose face had been ripped off by a bear, 21 years earlier, which I had painstakingly tried to repair. From there he was taken to our old home, before being feasted in the Officers' Mess. He stayed at a "hotel" in Dharan bazaar, to leave the following morning, on a bus for Kathmandu, a ten hour journey. A week later came the earthquake. The hotel was razed.

The hospital is now a Medical School – one of five in Nepal.

The Royal Family was massacred in 2001 by Crown Prince Dipendra, when they would not accept his intended fiancée. The official account was that he shot himself to die fourty eight hours later.

King Gyanendra (and Queen Komal) have never been popular since his brother's death and this led to a resurgence of the 7 year "People's War" which claimed 8000 lives before a fragile ceasefire was agreed in 2002. The Maoists now forcibly abduct children to fight for them. Bank robberies, extortion and "tax-levying" have amassed huge sums of money. Their red banner proclaims: "No to foreign intervention. Down with US imperialism". Many of us witnessed the total disruption of recruiting by the Maoists, filmed by Michael Palin's team, for the BBC production "Himalaya". On that occasion, recruiting had to be abandoned with crest fallen Gurkhas returning to their villages. The press reported the abduction of British Army Officers (released forty eight hours later).

American aid projects are now a target, with British development projects at risk, all very reminiscent of post war Iraq of 2005.

"The greatest danger is that Nepal could become a Sino-Indian football".

Massive bridges have been built over the vast rivers opening up East – West highways with roads from Nepalganj in the West leading to Bhairawa, Butwal, Pokhara, Kathmandu, Okhaldhunga, Taplejung, Ilam, Dhankuta and Dharan in the East.

*   *   *   *   *

When I left the army, I assisted my father, Norman, as his Registrar, at Redhill County Hospital, Smallfields and Crawley, for his last eighteen months in the NHS.

I then worked under Sir Hedley Atkins, President of the Royal College of Surgeons of England and Mr Frank Ellis, at Guy's, as Senior Registrar, and later for Mr Max Pemberton at

Chase Farm, Enfield. I was appointed Consultant Surgeon to the Havering Trust in 1972, working at Oldchurch, Rush Green, Victoria and Harold Wood hospitals.

We lived first in Bell Street, Reigate, then Gordon Hill, Enfield and next Lake Rise, Romford.

Anna, without Doma to help, had three children under five. Her patience, kindness, generosity and wisdom have rescued me from many difficult situations arising from my irascible nature.

I was invited to join the Territorial Army as a Regimental Medical Officer to the Royal Corps of Transport, serving for twenty-five years, including spells in Hong Kong, Indonesia, Burma, Korea and the Falklands.

We now live at Garnish Hall, Margaret Roding, near Dunmow, sharing the grounds with ducks, bantams, geese and black swans, badgers and deer.

James is a Colo-rectal Surgeon at Ipswich and I occasionally assist him with major rectal operations. He married Amanda Everett and they have three daughters: Daisy, Flora and Ella.

Rachel, Head Girl at St. Felix, Southwood, gained an honours degree in Manufacturing Engineering and Management at Loughborough University where she met and later married David Elliott. She took up accountancy and they have two children: Jonathan and Anna.

Betty Pratt, Anna's mother, died in 2001 at the age of 94 and "Jazz", her son, was honoured for his work in forestry with the M.B.E.

GLOSSARY

Carrying a basket and sporting a haemangioma, a blood vessel tumour, (over left eye).

Glossary

A.A.F.B.	Acid and Alcohol Fast Bacillus, (tuberculosis).
Achromycin	A form of Oxytetracycline, discontinued in July 2002.
Afterbirth, placenta	A vascular organ that connects the unborn baby to the womb and thereby supplies its nutrition.
Antibiotics	Group of drugs which kill specific micro-organisms.
Antibodies	Protective bodies in the blood of immune people.
Anticonvulsants	Drugs used to prevent fitting.
Antiseptics	Agents that kill bacteria.
Arthritis, Septic	Bacterial infection of a joint.
Ascites	Free fluid in the abdominal cavity.
A.T.S.	Anti-tetanus serum.
Bahadur	Brave man, warrior, commonest first name.
Bahun	Hindu tribe of Indian descent.
Bhag	Member of the large cat family.
Bhalu	A bear.
Bidi	Cigarette.
Bazaar	Township, collection of shops.
B.M.H.	British Military Hospital.
B.O.A.C.	British Overseas Airways Corporation
Bone marrow	Substance contained in the medullary cavity of bones, may be red or yellow. The red blood cells are produced by the red marrow.
Bronchus	Main airway to a lung.
Burn contracture	Scarring up after a burn.
Cannula	A tube for introduction into the body (usually into a vein).

Cantonment	The whole British camp at Dharan.
Chettri	Hindu tribe of Indian descent.
Chloramphenicol	Antibiotic used mostly for typhoid fever.
Cirrhosis	A disease of the liver resulting in severe scarring of the organ.
Colles fracture	Broken wrist.
Contracture	Fibrosis of muscle or connective tissue producing shrinkage and shortening.
Convulsion	An involuntary spasm or contraction of muscle.
Cross match	An examination that determines the safety of a blood transfusion.
C.S.S.D.	Central Sterile Supply Department.
Dahl	Lentils.
D & C	Dilation and curettage, method used to evacuate the uterus (womb).
Dashera	Head-cutting Nepalese festival.
Dextran	An emergency substitute for blood.
Dextrose	Sugar solution, safe to give as a transfusion.
Dewali	Festival of Lights.
Dhobi	Washerman.
Dialysis	Method of separating particles of different dimensions in a liquid mixture, using a thin semipermeable membrane to clear the blood of toxic products.
Doli	Hammock.
Drip	Another term for a transfusion.
Duca	Pain.
Empyema	Pus between the lung and chest wall.
Endemic disease	One to which the inhabitants of a particular district are peculiarly subject, affecting great numbers.
Encapsulated	An organ or tumour enclosed in a capsule.
Epidemic	Affecting great numbers.

Ergometrine	A drug whose specific action is to cause the womb to contract.
External cardiac massage	Production of a heart beat by intermittent pressure on the chest wall.
Femur	Thigh bone.
Fibula	Smaller of the two leg bones, the other being the tibia.
Flavine	Yellow antiseptic agent.
Foetal distress	The condition of the unborn baby is getting serious.
G.O.R. ward	Gurkha Other Rank ward.
Goitre	Swelling of the thyroid gland (in the neck).
Gurung	Tribe from which recruits are sought for the British Army.
Haematoma	Blood clot.
Haemoglobin	The pigment in the red cell which carries oxygen.
Haemostasis	Method of stopping bleeding.
Hookworm	Tiny worm that inhabits the duodenum and can cause profound anaemia.
Humerus	Upper arm bone between shoulder and elbow joint.
Hydatid cyst	A collection of fluid that is part of the life cycle of a worm.
Hydrocortisone	Drug used for resuscitation.
I.N.A.H.	Isoniazid. Drug used in the treatment of tuberculosis.
Immunity	Resistance to a disease, sometimes acquired by having already had the disease, or by injections to prevent the disease.

Infestation	Presence of animal parasites on skin or inside the body.
Intravenous	Situated within the vein.
I.V.P	Intravenous pyelogram, a succession of x-ray films of the urinary tract, following the injection into a vein of an iodine containing substance (which is opaque to x-rays). Now termed I.V.U. (Intravenous Urogram).
Intubate	The introduction of a tube into either a blood vessel or the larynx.
Kala-Azar	A parasite disease, involving especially the liver and spleen, resulting from the bite of a sand-fly.
Kapok	White fluffy material from the large seeds of a tree.
Kosi	Huge river fifteen miles east of the camp.
Küntscher nail	Long piece of metal used to fix a broken thigh bone.
Kukri	A knife, the national weapon.
Laparotomy	Exploratory operation to ascertain the diagnosis and carry out treatment whenever possible.
Largactil	A phenothiazine with pronounced sedative and autonomic effects.
Leech	An aquatic worm which sucks blood.
Limbu	Tribe from which recruits are sought for the British Army.
Macerated	Breaking up, rotting.
Malaria	A feverish disease with profound anaemia resulting from the bite of a certain mosquito.
Medullary cavity	The hollow in the centre of a long bone containing bone marrow.
Membrane	A thin layer of tissue that covers an organ.

Meniscectomy	Removal of torn cartilage usually from inside knee.
M.R.S.	Medical Reception Station, a miniature hospital.
Multigravida (Grand)	Pregnant with sixth or subsequent baby.
Namaste	Indian and Nepalese greeting with the hands placed as if in prayer.
Obstructed Labour	A block in the birth canal.
Oesophagus	Gullet.
Omentum	An apron of fat that lies across the intestines.
Osteomyelitis	Invasion of bone and marrow by disease producing micro-organisms.
Oxytetracycline	An antibiotic often used for cases in which penicillin has failed.
Palpation	Examination by pressure with the hand.
P.A.S.	Para-Aminosalicylic Acid. Drug used in the treatment of tuberculosis.
Peritoneum	Membrane that lines the abdominal walls and the contained organs.
Peritonitis	Inflammation of the peritoneum.
Pethidine	Pain-killing drug to which addiction can develop.
Phenobarbitone	Sedative, frequently used to prevent epileptic or other convulsions.
Pice	One tenth of a rupee.
Placenta	The afterbirth.
Placenta, retained	The afterbirth that has not delivered.
Plasma	Blood from which the red cells have been removed.
Prophylactic	Tending to ward off disease.
Protozoa	A group of microscopic single-celled animals. Some are disease causing parasites

of man e.g. Leishmania which causes Kala-azar.

Q.A.R.A.N.C.	Queen Alexandra's Royal Army Nursing Corps.
R.A.M.C.	Royal Army Medial Corps.
Rabies	A lethal virus disease contracted from mad dogs, wild animals and bats.
Rai	Tribe from which recruits are sought for the British Army.
Rakshi	A rum.
Reception	Where out-patients and emergencies are seen.
Red Guards	Maoist agitators in Hong Kong.
Renal failure	Relating to or affecting the kidneys.
Resuscitation	Treatment of shocked patients.
Roundworm	Worm, like an earthworm, that lives in the intestines.
Rupee	Coin, value approximately one shilling (5p).
Ryle's tube	A thin tube that can be passed through the nose or mouth into the stomach. Also termed naso-gastric.
Sari	Form of dress worn by the women.
Scaphoid	Small wrist bone, in the hollow, at the base of the thumb.
Septicaemia	Pus in the blood.
Serum	The fluid that separates from clotted blood.
Shaft of a bone	The long straight part of a bone.
Shikara	A skiff.
Shresta	Nepalese tribe.
Sindur	A dye used for haemostasis; can be yellow or red. When red can be used as a lipstick.
Smallpox	Severe virus disease characterised by a pustular rash.

Spleen	A vascular organ situated in the left upper abdomen.
Steimann pin	Small metal rod that is inserted through the tibia or the heel bone to help in traction for a broken femur or tibia.
Stethoscope	Instrument used by doctors to listen to the heart or abdomen.
Stilboestrol	A female hormone used to suppress lactation.
Streptomycin	An antibiotic usually used in the treatment of tuberculosis.
Sulphonomides	A group of antibacterial drugs used mostly for bladder and bowel infections.
Tamang	Tribe from which recruits are sought for the British Army.
Terai	Extensions of the plains of India.
Tetanus	A disease characterised by spasm and rigidity of the muscles of the body, caused by the contamination of a wound with *Clostridium tetani*, a bacteria found in manure and the soil.
Tharu	Aborigine tribe inhabiting the *terai*.
Thyroid	Gland lying in the neck across the trachea.
Tibia	The larger of the two bones of the lower leg between the knee and ankle.
Tola	A weight for gold equal to 180 grams troy (5,760 grams-one ounce).
Trachea	Windpipe.
Tracheostomy	Production of a hole in the outside of the windpipe.
Traction	Pulling on a fracture.
Transfusion	The introduction of blood or other fluid into the circulation, usually by a cannula into a vein.

Typhoid	An acute infectious disease involving the intestines; haemorrhage and perforation may complicate the disease.
Vaccinia	Very mild symptoms of smallpox, more like cowpox or chicken pox.
Villagers' clinic	A twice-weekly clinic held entirely for the natives of Nepal.